A TRAILS BOOKS GUIDE

GREAT WISCONSIN TAVERNS

101 DISTINCTIVE BADGER BARS

DENNIS BOYER

TRAILS BOOKS
Madison, Wisconsin

Library of Congress Catalog Card Number: 99-73862
ISBN: 0-915024-76-4

Editor: Stan Stoga
Cover designer: Kathie Campbell
Cover photograph: Mark Lepinske
Part illustrations: Owen Coyle

Printed in the United States of America

08 07 06 05 04 03 02 01 00 99   5 4 3 2 1

Trails Media Group, Inc.
P.O. Box 5650 · Madison, WI 53705
(800) 236-8088 · e-mail: info@wistrails.com
www.wistrails.com

In Memory of the
Pinckney Street Hideaway,
Mother's Pub,
Cafe Melange,
Four Mile House,
Thunder Road,
and the pre-fire Crystal Corner

Contents

▼ ▼ ▼ ▼ ▼ ▼ ▼ ▼ ▼ ▼ ▼ ▼ ▼ ▼ ▼ ▼ ▼

▼ ▼ ▼ ▼ ▼ ▼ ▼ ▼ ▼ ▼ ▼ ▼ ▼ ▼ ▼ ▼ ▼ ▼

▼ ▼ ▼ ▼ ▼ ▼ ▼ ▼ ▼ ▼ ▼ ▼ ▼ ▼ ▼ ▼ ▼

Introduction

One could easily conclude that the compilation of an abridged Wisconsin tavern guide is the height of presumption. Wisconsin's 14,000-plus licensed establishments give the Badger state an incredible range of choices and settings. Our diverse ethnic mix and varied cultural landscape give us virtually every North American tavern variation except the Mississippi Delta juke joint (although a few Wisconsin places adopt some southern features). Even some facsimile western saloons and southwestern cantinas weigh in with in-use hitching rails and weather-beaten sombreros.

This range provides one of the chief challenges to pulling a guide together when space allows but for a hundred or so entries rather than thousands. In addition, the question of what is a tavern is not a settled matter. All manner of establishments serve beer and other alcoholic beverages. Some spots stretch our traditional vision of the tavern. Others playfully and creatively fuse tavern elements in a variety of hospitality settings.

My working definition of tavern—assembled in the process of compiling this guidebook and after much consultation with tavern sources— has as much to do with sociology as with physical setting and business structure. First and foremost, a tavern is a location in which regular patrons gather to share drinks and fellowship. This element of community is what gives the tavern its continuity with the *stube* in Germany and the pub in Ireland.

Most of us also expect a tavern to have a bar counter of some sort, with stools after a fashion. Some would be so particular as to say that an establishment is not a true tavern without a massive back bar, replete with mirrors, oak columns, and a reproduction of the famous dogs-cheating-at-poker painting. Others, of the minimalist school, require only cold beer, brandy, and a rough plank on which to sit or lean.

This guidebook adopts a great deal of elasticity in the definition of taverns. A few establishments included here might lack elements that purists deem essential. But all have that key ingredient of a regular crowd that gathers for socializing and imbibing. And, a few comments regarding subculture and rough language notwithstanding, all are places in which a new face is welcome.

Honesty compels an admission of what this guide is *not*. It is not an attempt to rank Wisconsin taverns. It is impossible to use the standards by which one might evaluate fine restaurants. Taverns included here are great Wisconsin taverns, but an effort to rank them is an exercise in the mathematics of apples and oranges—even though I couldn't resist taking a stab at a "Top Ten" list (see page 11). Rankings based solely on amenities, food, and beer selection would skew the guidebook toward southeast Wisconsin. An effort is made to achieve the geographic balance that will be helpful to the traveler. The entries are organized by the standard quadrants used by the Wisconsin Department of Tourism. To avoid a hint of favoritism, I organized the taverns within each quadrant in alphabetical order of the city or town in which they are located. Readers will detect, however, that I have my preferences (most "blues clubs" outside Milwaukee manage to squeeze into this guidebook).

Twenty years of travel throughout Wisconsin took me to about 2,000 taverns before I started this project. I visited about 300 more in the two years of compiling the guide. Many of the spots evoke warm memories of friends made and local legends told. While I may have grown fussier in preferences over the years, I can still report that I liked almost all of the taverns. My tavern journals contain only a few disparaging notations such as "should be burned, bulldozed, and turned into a parking lot."

The passage of time has brought many changes to the tavern industry. Simple ownership of a Wisconsin tavern is no longer a guaranteed license to print money. Regulatory burdens, drinking age changes, and tougher drunk-driving enforcement all combine to make life more complicated for the tavern owner. Many tavern owners feel that Native American gaming in the form of casinos has also diverted business. I saw no evidence of this, and by and large, the casino crowd is not a tavern crowd.

Another thing I noticed on my travels are the parallels between the tavern industry and Wisconsin's dairy farms. One major similarity is age demographics. Many owner/operators in both sectors are of retirement age. Some continue because of a genuine fondness for their vocation. Others hang on bitterly in the usually vain hope that if they wait, a sucker with wads of cash will show up to buy them out.

Chain or franchise tavern/restaurants also pop up to fuel the insecurity of mom-and-pop taverns. While none of the franchise places are included in the guide, it must be conceded that they generally do a good job. In our modern mobile society they fulfill the needs of those without community roots and those who like the comfortable guarantee that the setting will be similar in each location.

All the troubling trends aside, it could still be argued that Wisconsin is in the midst of a golden age of taverns and beer drinking. Young progressive owners have revitalized many a moribund spot. Places that stress customer satisfaction are thriving. The spread of microbreweries and brew pubs has done much to educate consumers. Indeed, the buildup of Wisconsin brew pubs, the number of which tripled in the last two years, complicated my guidebook task by threatening to displace the listings of more traditional rustic spots. I've attempted to recognize these newer establishments by reviewing some, in addition to compiling all of them in a separate list (see page 98). All are worthy of a visit.

A word is in order about beer terminology used in the guidebook. The terms *nationals, standards,* and *industrials* are used to describe the availability of the big brands like Miller and Budweiser. The label *regional* is meant to include

▼ ▼ ▼ ▼ ▼ ▼ ▼ ▼ ▼ ▼ ▼ ▼ ▼ ▼ ▼ ▼ ▼ ▼

Wisconsin's enduring hometown breweries such as Joseph Huber, Stevens Point, and Leinenkugel. The terms *microbrew* and *micros* embrace the brews from the specialty breweries devoted to the production of fine beers and ales in smaller batches. The term *craft brew* is used to denote the specialty beer produced by the larger breweries.

As happens with a project of this type, conditions change and businesses evolve or die. Follow-up efforts caught a few taverns that have closed or changed beyond recognition. Undoubtedly, there are tavern gems that escaped my attention. Updates, additions, and notice of significant changes from readers are welcome and can be sent to Trails Media Group, P.O. Box 5650, Madison, WI 53705.

Enjoy your tavern tours of Wisconsin. Our taverns are a unique part of our heritage and landscape. Cheers!

▼ ▼ ▼ ▼ ▼ ▼ ▼ ▼ ▼ ▼ ▼ ▼ ▼ ▼ ▼ ▼ ▼

Acknowledgments

The whole of tavern life is greater than the sum of its parts. But one of the weightiest components of our attraction to taverns is the warmth evoked by the memories of those who introduced us to its communal pleasures. For many generations, this remembrance could be traced to a combination of parental figures, village elders, blue-collar foremen, and crusty sergeants and petty officers.

Such is the legacy that brought me to this pleasurable task. My thanks go out to my father, Erwin Boyer, and my uncles, Harold Boyer, Jonathan Reinert, and Jess Choyce. A nod of the hod to George Minner, my first job-related tavern buddy.

A stiff salute to my main G.I. bar pals: Gene Levesque, Orland Taylor, and Robbie Robinson. Thanks for the memories of a thousand watering holes from the Anacostia Naval Yard to Bangkok. A toast to the ghosts of the Club Unique in Saigon—especially Phan Thi Net. And a flashed peace sign to Paul Fichter for shared beers in the war after the war and to his mom, Muriel, for allowing her basement to become a tavern for a very scruffy crowd.

A raised mason jar to my ridge runner guides in West Virginia: John Yeager, Tom Smith, Jim Dawson, Sylvia Geise, and Zeke Lahr. Hope you all gave up those "red eyes." A waved carman's light to the former Car Department of the Milwaukee Road at Portage, Wisconsin: Jerry Rosenow, Tony Hauser, Al Strayer, Auchie Zahn, and Babe Reardon.

Politics may make for strange bedfellows, but it makes for great pub pals. The usual suspects: Conrad Amenhauser, Tiny Wells, Marty Beil, Susan Lampert Smith, Phil Neuenfeldt, Ed Huck, Woody Welch, Sandy Bloomfield, Joe Looby, Tom Gerber, and Jennifer Grondin. I won't embarrass any public officials by naming them here.

The guidebook benefited from frequent consultation with a "kitchen cabinet" of tavern veterans: John Bergum (whose motor home and companionship kept me warm, dry, and in good humor on the road trips), Pat James, Dave Johnson, Mike Surtees, Bonita Rowland, Johna and Rick Borowitz, and Stu Becker.

Many friendly folks also steered me to uncharted taverns and gave me feedback on their own visitations: Bill Boyer, Lori Ahl, Robin Arnold, Bill Berry, Justin Isherwood, Liz McBride, Bryan and Susan Johnson, Sid Lepseier, Katrina Kinder, Courtney Monette, Scott Stenger, Frank Koehn, Jeff Platt, Kevin Traas, Brad Verhelst, Russ Moody, Robert White, Kathleen Haas, Michelle James, and the "staff" of Art's Performing Center.

Most of all, thanks to Donna. Couldn't do it without you.

Bless you all, each and every one.

Southeast
Wisconsin

▼ ▼ ▼ ▼ ▼ ▼ ▼ ▼ ▼ ▼ ▼ ▼ ▼ ▼ ▼ ▼ ▼ ▼

Make no mistake about it, the southeast section of the state is prime tavern country. Sure, the mention of Wisconsin might evoke an image of log taverns on mist-shrouded lakes. But southeast Wisconsin is the land of *Happy Days* and the Fonz, beers that made Milwaukee famous, machine shops, and is the home of Harley-Davidson, and a healthy mix of Holsteins, cheese factories, and small towns.

It is also one of the most ethnically German areas in North America. Before Prohibition it was a stronghold of local breweries that found homes in almost every community with more than a thousand people. It was also home to great brewing fortunes that left legacies in Milwaukee.

Some would say that southeast Wisconsin's peak tavern period came in the prosperous 1950s and 1960s when industrial giants like Allis-Chalmers, Caterpillar, and American Motors provided tens of thousands of decent-paying jobs. Neighborhood taverns thrived, as did the taverns across from plant gates and in or near the union halls. Entertainment options had not expanded to today's level and the generation gap had not created tavern turf wars. Live music was common in tavern venues and ranged from polkas to country and western to brand-new rock and roll. A generation of World War II veterans, flush with the happy swagger of taming a world gone mad, celebrated survival and hope for the future.

Wisconsin's tavern landscape changed with the social and economic changes of the 1970s and 1980s. Younger patrons sought out places where long hair and colorful clothing would not invite harassment. Many older taverns were remodeled as lounges and discos that drew upon urban nightclub traditions. Decline of heavy industry and creeping rust belt malaise cut heavily into the disposable income and optimism of the blue-collar sector.

These changes notwithstanding, the area is still one of the best places in North America to drink beer and visit taverns. Indeed, with its proliferation of brew pubs, spiffed-up microbrew bars, and rediscovered classic neighborhood taverns, one could easily conclude that southeast Wisconsin is the heartland of a tavern renaissance.

As with the other areas demarked by the Wisconsin Department of Tourism's regional divisions, the southeast part of the state presents a varied cultural geography. The lakeshore district of Sheboygan and Manitowoc closely resembles the industrial/maritime clusters one finds in parts of Michigan and Ohio. Milwaukee, of course, is as close as we get to big-city feel. Madison is in a category by itself as a government and academic center. The Lake Winnebago area, particularly the eastern shore, has a unique subculture of fishing and boating taverns. Throw in Kenosha, Racine, Janesville, and zones as varied as Lake Geneva, Wisconsin Dells, and Horicon Marsh, and you have a microcosm of the Upper Midwest.

Milwaukee and Madison could easily provide a sufficient number of notable taverns to merit guidebooks of their own. Both cities pose challenges to the compiler of a statewide guide by offering enough unique and well-appointed

▼ ▼ ▼ ▼ ▼ ▼ ▼ ▼ ▼ ▼ ▼ ▼ ▼ ▼ ▼ ▼ ▼ ▼

taverns to threaten to squeeze out rural and small-town taverns. Growing numbers of taverns in both cities pay close heed to contemporary consumer preferences. Both communities have many neighborhoods worthy of pub crawls.

Driving tours of rural taverns are not as compact or linear as in much of the rest of the state. The four-lane highways displaced many of the old roadhouses, while malls and suburban housing transformed the settings around others. Some travelers still favor the many rural and small-town taverns off the side roads of Highway 51 in Columbia County. Others prefer the Cambridge-Jefferson-Waukesha stretch of Highway 18. A unique trek in ice fishing season can be found on segments of Highways 151 and 55 that hug Lake Winnebago between Fond du Lac and Sherwood. So whether you're in the mood for big-city adventures or small-town hospitality (or anything in between), the southeast region has it all.

▼ ▼ ▼ ▼ ▼ ▼ ▼ ▼ ▼ ▼ ▼ ▼ ▼ ▼ ▼ ▼ ▼ ▼

Beloit

Suds O'Hanahan's Irish Pub
435 E. Grand Avenue
(608) 368-1933

Rock County is just starting to catch up with the beer craze and much of the education is occurring at Suds O'Hanahan's. At one time, Beloit had many more pleasant neighborhood taverns, but some neighborhoods have varying degrees of decay and the stressed-out bars have been slow to pick up on beer diversity. Still, there is a fine tavern tradition in Beloit that this pub manages to at once uphold and update.

Suds O'Hanahan's coolers hold a treasure of 50 bottled imports and domestics, with some emphasis as you might expect on the Emerald Isle. After a concession or two to our national brews, the taps give a tip of the hat in the same geographical direction, with Harp, Bass, and Guinness proudly flowing. The diverse crowd pulls in for sandwiches and snacks, too. The regulars include many border hoppers from Illinois. Many beer fanciers are drawn in by positive mentions of Suds O'Hanahan's on pub crawl websites and various beer-related publications. It's a worthy spot in Wisconsin's southern border county.

Our hardy team of tavern inspectors pronounced it their favorite Rock County watering hole on a 22-bar tour that spanned the distance from Edgerton to the Illinois line. It is worth mentioning that I was in the company of two veteran pub crawlers who've done their time at the General Motors assembly plant in Janesville. They related their assessment of tavern health in the area and painted a picture like that encountered in rapidly developing areas like the Fox Valley and Waukesha. They waxed nostalgic about the lost rural taverns and the run-down state of the factory-district bars. They even had a kind word or two to say about the 1960s and 1970s heyday of the area's supper clubs.

Neither of them saw their past favorites reincarnated in the form of Suds's, but they saw in this modern form a lot more hope for the tavern future than we found elsewhere that day. They groused a bit at the lack of places to spit their snuff juice, and they at first uttered snide epithets like "urban hip" and "yuppie beer emporium." Then they settled into the beer, the crowd, and the conversation. They were won over for good when a thirty-something kindergarten teacher explained the distinctions between ale and lager.

Watch out if some of the regulars suggest some spots for you to visit in cross-border South Beloit. Bartenders at Suds's said those forays are definitely a walk on the wild side.

▼ ▼ ▼ ▼ ▼ ▼ ▼ ▼ ▼ ▼ ▼ ▼ ▼ ▼ ▼ ▼ ▼ ▼

Winkers Tap
N8638 Market Street
(920) 689-2348

Winkers is what our mothers used to expect from a mom-and-pop tavern: clean Formica counters and scrubbed floors. On my first visit I sat and watched in awe as they washed the windows. Even the velvet paintings look dry-cleaned! Here is the antithesis of the seedy conditions found in far too many taverns. You know the type I'm referring to: dust on the potato chip bags, peeling linoleum floors, grimy cooking facilities, and restrooms that merit the donning of a chemical/biological warfare suit. Not at Winkers.

One might ask what would bring a traveler to Burnett other than random cruising. Well, for starters it is on the periphery of the Horicon Marsh area. The Wild Goose State Trail passes within fifty yards of the front door. In the summer months the daytime customers are fresh off the trail looking for cold pop and the unusual tavern offering of Schwann's ice cream. Autumn visitors stop for beer, brandy, directions, and reports on the geese.

It's not uncommon for waterfowl hunters to stop in, too. Even the occasional wildlife manager drops in to wet the whistle and ground the goose lore in a dose of scientific fact. Some great seasoned outdoors storytellers were known to frequent this spot at one time. Many have passed on. But there is still the one up-in-years fellow who will recount a 1940s bitter autumn storm, with full dramatic narrative of the deaths of waterfowl hunters caught out on lakes that day. His stories of frostbite, exposure, howling winds, and frozen bodies had me feeling cold enough to order up a brandy on a July afternoon.

While I often bemoan limited beer selections and scant amenities in small taverns, Winkers is living proof of the beauty of simplicity. Miller beer and Pepsi comprise the bulk of refreshments. A short bar is supplemented by a few tables. The old-style jukebox and the pool table are the only rainy-day distractions other than watching the occasional Wisconsin and Southern train rumble by. But it is still a nice fit for those who can't part with their broken-in hiking boots or other things that have grown comfortable and familiar.

Local residents sometimes use Winkers as a starting point before an evening out. On Friday nights, before the trip to the fish fry, a few drinks are in order. Then comes the 100-yard stroll across the trail and the tracks to Theide's Tavern for catfish and Rolling Rock. A nice little tandem visit!

▼ ▼ ▼ ▼ ▼ ▼ ▼ ▼ ▼ ▼ ▼ ▼ ▼ ▼ ▼ ▼ ▼ ▼

Chilton

The Roll Inn (at Rowland's Calumet Brewing Company)
25 N. Madison Street
(920) 849-2534

If you love beer, you must meet Bob Rowland. There are few tavern hosts who rival Bob's congeniality and outright exuberance. What Wisconsin governor Tommy Thompson is to Badger State boosterism, Bob Rowland is to the cause of good beer. I have not met the *Homo sapiens* who has a bad word to say about him, unless you count the comments that his spouse is even nicer.

Aside from running one of the smallest (and the most off the beaten track) brew pubs in North America, Bob hosts the annual Wisconsin Microbrewers Fest at the Calumet County fairgrounds. His cheerful face is a regular feature at other microbrew events. Some say that a Wisconsin brew fest does not even count if Bob and his beers do not make an appearance.

The pub and brewery are in a former fire station with a sturdy ragtime-era feel. Owner confidence and customer loyalty allow the Roll Inn to offer only their five year-round brews and three seasonals (including a unique rye beer) as on-premise beverages. They underline that straight-up beer statement with an emphatic no-menu stance.

While somewhat of a hidden jewel, the Roll Inn has since its 1990 opening garnered an extensive word-of-mouth following. It has many local regulars but also boasts an incredible draw of outsiders. During my last visit, the vehicles in the parking lot sported license plates from California, Indiana, Ontario, South Dakota, and Utah. Not to mention a stretch limo from Milwaukee with four beer fanatics.

It goes without saying that such a spot, under the auspices of such a warm and knowledgeable host, would brew up some great beer stories. Is the Pope Catholic? Does a bear relieve itself in the woods? Yes, the beer talk is about as deep as it can get on this earthly plane and on occasion transcends the gap between mortal brewers and the angels who guard the blessed beverage.

I am not exaggerating when I say that beer is treated with reverence here. There are thirsty pilgrims who sojourn here who see a sacredness in beer that is positively tribal in its spirituality. One such apostle held me spellbound with a lengthy psalm of beer's connection to ancient rites, shamanism, healing, herbalism, and magic. Before he was done I could experience in a good beer the legacy of druids and medicine men and women. He predicted a time when beer will again be brewed that lets us commune with the Divine. Holy beer stein!

▼ ▼ ▼ ▼ ▼ ▼ ▼ ▼ ▼ ▼ ▼ ▼ ▼ ▼ ▼ ▼ ▼

Delafield
Carpenter's Pub
603 Genesee Street
(262) 646-4899

rish music, food, and beer give this spot a wee bit of the Emerald Isle feel. Yet Carpenter's Pub is becoming a regional draw based on its no smoking policy. Tavern owners take note: this establishment has experienced as much as 50% annual sales increases based on the fact that many consumers would love to sample good beer without incurring lung damage or stinking up their wardrobes. Every community that can support a dozen or more taverns should be able to sustain one smoke-free beer joint.

The tap system usually offers at least ten different draft brews. Murphy's, Harp, and Newcastle are big sellers, but Leinenkugel's line holds its own. The coolers hold approximately fifty different brands. Imports move more quickly here than in most Wisconsin taverns, although the regulars discovered New Glarus beer before the rest of southeast Wisconsin. The steady crowd likes the anticipation of waiting for new beers to crop up for their drinking pleasure.

The weekends bring music. Mostly Irish and bluegrass. Summer brings larger crowds to an outside deck. The menu consists of simple but sturdy fare. There are sandwiches and a fish fry. The real treats come in the form of Irish stew in stout and shepherd's pie. Both of these dishes made a big impression with me and are worth a stop even if you hate taverns and despise beer.

The combination of all the aforementioned factors creates an environment where Carpenter's can thrive by attracting those who drink one or two beers and by turning over the customers almost hourly. This is not to say that it is an establishment without regulars. No, this tavern has an assortment of characters that would do any Dublin pub proud. But most of the people here are on the go.

One advantage to that mobility and active engagement with life is the ability of many customers of Carpenter's to refer the wayfarer to other suitable taverns. Unlike a lot of beer drinkers in southeast Wisconsin, patrons here break out of that parochial three- or four-neighborhood-tavern repertoire.

Carpenter's Pub often operates on "European hours," closing between 2 P.M. and 5 P.M.. They are closed Sundays. A call ahead is strongly suggested.

Fond du Lac

The Main Pub
6th & Main Streets
(920) 924-7815

Picking a Fond du Lac tavern for this guide proved to be one of the more difficult tasks. This city at the base of Lake Winnebago has an abundance of neighborhood bars and a number of interesting clusters. Part of the difficulty came from the loss of a number of favorites (chief among them the Four Mile House, a venerable roadhouse on Highway 151 south) in the last few years. When a tavern that's been under your skin for two decades bites the dust it's like losing an old friend. But it also reminds you that your friendship with that one spot has kept you out of circulation.

In Fond du Lac, that meant a fresh reconnaissance mission to the downtown Main Street tavern district, an area that a decade ago definitely lacked the easy sociability of the old neighborhood taverns, the character of the west shore fishing bars, and the down-home atmosphere of the country bars on the fringe of the city. Those places are now often closed or have fallen on hard times. It is Main Street that is making a comeback, and the Main Pub is leading the way.

There are very few spots that pack as much in a small space as the Main Pub. It's kind of a narrow dining car configuration, with a bar of generous length and some island-counter seating. Throw in a pool table, two dartboards, a pinball machine, a golf machine, and a massive jukebox and you're in for a tight fit on a crowded weekend night. But if you're over 40 those are nights to avoid anyway, as the average age dips down into the early 20s and is not at all beer savvy considering the on-premises resources. We of the middle years do well to stop in on weekdays after 4 P.M. That's when the crowd is at its diverse best.

And what a nice crowd! The folks lean toward the blue-collar side, with representation of construction workers, local government employees, postal workers, health care employees, and quite a few single parents and older students. Conversations turned up a poet, a few musicians, lots of sports enthusiasts, a couple boaters, and a young Maori woman from New Zealand with a story to tell as warm as her smile.

This is the beer crowd. They account for the coolers stocked with over 50 imports and micros. They prompt the steady pull of the eight taps. The lineups are not exotic but have good representation of various brew types. Of note are the bottles of McEwans Scotch Ale and the oft-tapped Hacker-Pschorr Weisse

▼ ▼ ▼ ▼ ▼ ▼ ▼ ▼ ▼ ▼ ▼ ▼ ▼ ▼ ▼ ▼ ▼ ▼

and Leinie's Berry Weiss. It's also the cigar crowd, with the Don Tomas and As-tral brands bearing most of the traffic. Women join in on this puffing, too.

The friendly atmosphere on weekday evenings merits a visit if you're in the area. But the crowd-shy can safely visit on Saturdays before the evening really gets cooking. You might even mix in with a crowd of regulars that forsakes the bar in mid-evening and invites whoever is handy out to a lakeside bonfire.

▼ ▼ ▼ ▼ ▼ ▼ ▼ ▼ ▼ ▼ ▼ ▼ ▼ ▼ ▼ ▼ ▼

Germania (south of Neshkora)

Longbranch Saloon
W 1936 Eagle Road
(920) 293-8448

A friend called the Longbranch "a quirky curio shop of a bar." While the name conjures up images of Wild West cattle drives and gunfights, the atmosphere is pure Wisconsin marsh country. Speaking of which, the Longbranch squats at the edge of the Germania Marsh State Wildlife Area like a fat bullfrog.

The area is home to some of the strangest ghost stories in the state and has its share of tall tales. One Longbranch regular whispered an odd tale of amorous spirits that visit in the night to consummate their love of living flesh. This account gave new meaning to the phrase "they all look prettier at closing time" and reduced my inclination to take him up on his offer to let me pitch my tent on his spit of land out in the marsh. Another talked of a local variation on Bigfoot. Then there are the fifty-year-old stories of flying saucers. Hey, they're just getting started.

This is home of the "Hippo Burger" and therein lies one of Wisconsin's strangest legends. A decade ago, fishermen in the area were accused of mental disorder and intoxication when they reported seeing a full-grown hippopotamus in local rivers and swamps. It turned out the critter had escaped from a game farm. Ultimately the animal was destroyed after capture efforts failed. Thus the "Hippo Burger." No one is talking if indeed a hippo haunch still occupies a freezer locker.

There is a small colony of Madison East Siders who park RVs and trailers in the area and add to the local color. Just make sure that if any Longbranch storytellers are holding court that they do not turn out to be Madison cabdrivers. They love to pull the chains of casual passersby and act the part of the backwoods yahoo.

While microbrews and imports have not reached into this bit of marsh country, the standard beers are available in around 15 varieties. The locally acclaimed fish fry brings in a mixed crowd of local families, grubby fishermen, and weekend visitors. It's a congenial mixture and is remembered fondly by those whose travels bring them to Germania on an infrequent basis. Kids and adults alike are captivated by the heavily visited bird feeders near an outside deck. Closed Mondays.

▼ ▼ ▼ ▼ ▼ ▼ ▼ ▼ ▼ ▼ ▼ ▼ ▼ ▼ ▼ ▼ ▼ ▼ ▼

ANOTHER ROUND
Boyer's Top Ten Taverns

A list of preferences or rankings is, of course, a highly personal and subjective process. But since I have already disclosed my leanings and background elsewhere in this guidebook, I feel I can offer the following lineup in the spirit of fun and good-natured argument over many a brew:

1. Witz End—Stevens Point
2. Zur Krone—Milwaukee
3. Bodega Brew Pub—La Crosse
4. Holly Rocks—Wisconsin Rapids
5. Molly's Grill—Black River Falls
6. Harmony Bar and Grill—Madison
7. Pat and Mike's—Dodgeville
8. Anchor Bar and Grill—Superior
9. The Roll Inn—Chilton
10. Scott Street Steak and Pub—Wausau

▼ ▼ ▼ ▼ ▼ ▼ ▼ ▼ ▼ ▼ ▼ ▼ ▼ ▼ ▼ ▼ ▼ ▼

Green Lake

The Goose Blind
512 Gold Street
(920) 294-6363

The Goose Blind's management doesn't call attention to its bar area. All the billing goes to its casual dining. Maybe this is a move calculated to keep out the riffraff. Wait a minute, Green Lake has no riffraff! This is definitely not a stop on motorcycle club bar tours. The spot is an entirely modern version of Green Lake's acclaimed Victorian-era hospitality and brings in families from Chicago who maintain fourth- and fifth-generation ties to this resort community.

But it should be a stop on craft brew and microbrew tours. The Goose Blind keeps 12 taps pumping with various brews from Berghoff, Gray's, Sprecher, and Leinenkugel. The bottled-beer list has 30 brands, including many micros and imports. In addition, bartenders get plenty of practice at mixing cocktails. The suds tapper on duty during my last visit claimed to have a repertoire of six different old-fashioneds.

Comfort is the watchword here. No duct-taped barstools; high padded swivel captain's chairs serve the bar. Well-arranged booths and café tables provide additional seating in the bar. A cozy screened-in porch and second-story deck round out the spots to relax. The mood is subdued here, and this is definitely not the type of place where a rebel yell will net you a free drink. Yet the customers are always sociable. It's a suitable place to go for a genteel moment after a stint in a no-holds-barred juke joint.

On a slow day it is often possible to persuade one of the white-haired eminences to talk of that time of wooden rowboats, gentlemen in hats and long-sleeved white shirts rowing, and ivory-skinned ladies hiding beneath parasols. If the stories can be believed, those nineteenth-century ways lasted nearly up to World War II in Green Lake. It's a mood that is still detectable in this community and in this establishment.

Customers range from local professionals to upscale resort patrons. Many are nondrinkers drawn in by the extensive menu. In the bar, the hearty sandwiches, distinctive homemade pizzas, and Mexican specialties keep palates happy.

▼ ▼ ▼ ▼ ▼ ▼ ▼ ▼ ▼ ▼ ▼ ▼ ▼ ▼ ▼ ▼ ▼

Hartford (St. Lawrence)

Rothaus
4900 Highway 175
(262) 644-8181

Change is the watchword at the Rothaus. Formerly the Little Red Inn, the spot already had a following for Red Brick ales and food. The Germanic conversion means a shift to traditional German lagers and German cuisine. More than one of my sources also favorably cited a renewed level of service and hospitality.

The kickoff for the new identity came in late 1998 with the production of Rothaus Octoberfest and Rothaus Helles (a blonde lager). By the time you read this, more brews will have poured forth. Robert Wilber, co-owner and brewer, expects to draw upon experience gained in apprenticeships at Wurtzburger and Braueri Friedmann in Germany to produce very traditional beer. The response by microfans to these efforts has been very positive. Some of my fussiest beer buddies pronounce Rothaus brews among the best brew pub products in the Midwest.

The menu hails from central Germany, tipping off the Thuringian training of the chef. Lots of pork, lots of garlic, cream sauces, sauerbraten, and potato dumplings. Don't miss the beer sauces! It is quite a compliment to a kitchen in a transition business that it manages to hold on to its past loyalists while winning over a whole new batch. Those whose tastes run to the Germanic side of beverages and edibles will be hard-pressed to find a better one-two combination. Those familiar with the cuisine of central Germany pronounced it very true to form. The beer backers here told me I should not plug the food lest the spot be overrun by mere diners. Sorry, guys.

Also of note in this transition period is the appearance of a large display of German brewery and beer-drinking artifacts. Many of the items are rare and of historic interest to the beer-inclined. This in turn has spun off a modest group of beer-memorabilia devotees who have declared this their home base. Thus one can eavesdrop here on the Milwaukee area's growing effort to create a national beer museum.

▼　▼　▼　▼　▼　▼　▼　▼　▼　▼　▼　▼　▼　▼　▼　▼　▼　▼

Janesville

Hilltop Pub and Grill

123 E. Milwaukee Street

(608) 758-0809

Janesville represents a mainstream America that might be seen as an update of Norman Rockwell's portrayals of community life. As such, it does not cultivate a reputation as a drinking town, but neither does it harbor the prudish outlook of the previously "dry" communities of nearby southwest Wisconsin.

The Hilltop is a good fit for rock-solid, truck-building Janesville. A well-respected and reasonably priced ($7.95) pot roast dinner, a famous Deluxe Burger, and a mix of national, regional, and local brews make it a favorite spot for both General Motors and government office workers. So it was with some pleasure that this union man was put in a position to argue about both the various regional beers and the major Wisconsin unions. The discussion was fun, but neither dispute was brought to conclusion. That's the beauty of a tavern discussion; it lives for another day and another beer.

Definitely not a "beer snob" bar, the Hilltop serves as a neighborhood tavern for nearby neighborhoods that developed without taverns. It also anchors a downtown that is without a true tavern district. But it is within walking distance of a few other clean and friendly bars. And it should be mentioned that Janesville's taverns are a generally decent lot, even if thought to be too white-bread by two-fisted types and those with a penchant for sleazy gin mills. Hey, this is Janesville.

The Hilltop is a good spot to hear acoustic guitar music. Sometimes there are even performances on weeknights. It's an intimate bar setting with limited seating. So come early on weekend nights. The lively talk about sports, cars, and music is at the bar. Couples, music lovers, and chowhounds occupy the tables. A surprising number of customers here told me that they rarely go into any taverns other than the Hilltop. Even a few Dane County folks are known to slip down to Janesville to relax in this wholesome spot (only in Janesville would the label "wholesome" not act to drive customers away from a tavern).

The big party night of the year is Halloween. It's a Hilltop tradition, with special food and music. Try the "witch's brew." Here the stories are not about ghosts, but about people who partied too hearty and thought they saw ghosts.

▼ ▼ ▼ ▼ ▼ ▼ ▼ ▼ ▼ ▼ ▼ ▼ ▼ ▼ ▼ ▼ ▼

Brewmasters Brew Pub
4017 80th Street (south of Highway 50)
(262) 694-9050

Brewmasters Northside
1170 22nd Avenue (near UW-Parkside)
(262) 552-2805

OK, I admit it. I'm trying to sneak a few extra watering holes into the guide. But I have a perfect cover for this sneakiness. The businesses are under the same ownership and brew masters. Not to mention that they are twins in the matters of quality and followings. This is a trend that I've failed to note elsewhere: those who get it right in the tavern business are often exactly the right people to open another operation.

My second excuse is that the 80th Street location was the first brew pub in heartland America. At the time of the 1987 opening, on-premises tavern brewing was strictly an East Coast/West Coast phenomenon. We always owe a debt of gratitude to our pioneer forebears.

As if that were not enough to earn Brewmasters a spot in the annals of Wisconsin tavern history, there are the unique circumstances surrounding the start-up at the 22nd Avenue site. Not only is the new brewing facility a state-of-the-art system, but it is infused with Kenosha pride. Dozens of local craftsmen and companies helped with design and set-up. Only in skilled blue-collar Kenosha would you hear steamfitters and machinists mixing beer talk with engineering specifications.

Oh, by the way, the beer also bears the marks of this skill and caring. Over 30 brews are crafted in the course of a year. Few brew pubs approach this variety. Southeast Wisconsin beer fanatics favor the Irish Mocha Stout. My palate was tickled by the Doppelbock. These places have an extremely ambitious brew agenda. But the loyalists, who hail from Burlington, Racine, and northern Illinois, feel that there are more hits than misses. Real trailblazers are always risk takers. Join them in a beer adventure.

Food is also served Kenosha style: calzones, pizzas, pasta, seafood, steaks, brats, and chops. The 80th Street location has a comfortable-shoe feel. The 22nd Avenue site has more bustle, including a 300-seat banquet hall.

▼ ▼ ▼ ▼ ▼ ▼ ▼ ▼ ▼ ▼ ▼ ▼ ▼ ▼ ▼ ▼ ▼ ▼

Kenosha

Ron's Place
3301 52nd Street
(262) 657-5907

Welcome to Wisconsin! This is a frequent introductory stop for our neighboring flatlanders and other visitors to our fair state. Two of the reasons that the fine Illinois folks like to stop in are the good beer and the friendly Wisconsinites. But they keep coming back because of a variety of elements having to do with the Wisconsin tavern mystique. Many such visitors think of Ron's as the traditional urban Wisconsin tavern. It's so much more than that, but why mess with their belief systems? It thankfully is not even a representative Kenosha tavern, many of which came through the 1980s decline a little worse for wear.

Ron's represents that part of Kenosha that bounced back. Some parts did, some didn't. Let's face it, much of Kenosha feels like Illinois. Some even feels like the Bronx. By gosh, you can find Cubs and Bears fans here, and even White Sox fans. White Sox fans! So we can forgive them if they don't know much about Wisconsin north of Highway 11, much less Highway 2.

But Ron's can't be faulted on the beer and hospitality end. They run ten taps balanced with national, regional, and imports. The bottled selection ebbs and flows but seems to always have at least 15 imports. Ron's Place has a reputation for good bartenders and sociable customers. So some of us in Wisconsin reverse the pattern used by Illinois visitors: stop here and take a deep breath before you go on to Chicago.

There's a Madison group that occasionally makes a southeast Wisconsin loop on their way to Cubs games and allows me to ride shotgun on their interstate pub crawl. They are of the belief that it is an absolute ethical necessity to have a last drink at Ron's, in deference to Wisconsin loyalty, to gird their loins against the city masses to the south. They regale the Illinois visitors with bizarre Ed Gein stories and other legends of the Wisconsin wilds. In general they attempt to reinforce every negative stereotype that an urbanite might have about rural life. I hate to break it to them, but I think the city slickers are on to the fact that these Madison "woodsmen" are all desk jockeys with graduate degrees.

▼ ▼ ▼ ▼ ▼ ▼ ▼ ▼ ▼ ▼ ▼ ▼ ▼ ▼ ▼ ▼ ▼

Madison

Cardinal Bar
418 E. Wilson Street
(608) 251-0800

In some circles the label "activist hangout" is a dismissive epithet. In Madison it is more likely to suggest lively entertainment and a social conscience. The Cardinal has been a gathering spot for gays and lesbians for years, but its eclectic offerings and the civic activism of owner Ricardo Gonzalez has made it a community institution that is fondly regarded by a host of progressive constituencies. It is difficult to tally the numbers of Madisonians with good things to say about the Cardinal. And for a multitude of reasons.

The Cardinal has hosted countless political fund-raisers and benefits over the last two decades. Yet among nonactivists, the lively nightspot is known more for its dance club side than its politics. Specialty nights are heavy on Latin, swing, and disco. It can be depended on to run early-evening lessons whenever new dance crazes hit town. Celebrity DJs often pick the tunes and get to spin their favorite music for their favorite causes. "Fetish Night" is no longer the local sensation it was when first unleashed, but leather-laden lads and lassies still cut loose and raise the eyebrows of staid passersby.

A classic bar area shows signs of tasteful renovation. Local micros and imports get good billing. Bartenders have a top-notch reputation for cocktails and specialty drinks. The martini drinkers among my circle tell me the Cardinal's is among the best three or four in Madison. Señor Gonzalez's Cuban roots show up in periodic cigar nights.

Madison has lost many of the bars associated with its antiwar glory days. Spots like the now-departed 602 Club were as much a part of the young adulthood of the student movement as the USO and military post clubs were for their parents' generation. The Cardinal is one of the few places where you might run into someone who could tell you about the war at home, the freedom rides, the Madison newspaper strike, and the host of peace and social-justice groups that blossomed in Madison in the 1970s and 1980s. While the level of activism is no longer at the boiling-over point, the Cardinal still reminds many of us of those times when we thought we could change the world and sort of did change it.

▼ ▼ ▼ ▼ ▼ ▼ ▼ ▼ ▼ ▼ ▼ ▼ ▼ ▼ ▼ ▼ ▼ ▼

Madison

Harmony Bar and Grill
2201 Atwood Avenue
(608) 249-4333

Analyzed in sociological and folklore journals, praised by restaurant critics, beloved by fans of blues and roots rock, and just plain appreciated by beer drinkers, the Harmony occupies a special niche in Madison's tavern pantheon. It pulls off the trick of serving as a neighborhood tavern and a citywide/regional nightspot. It also bridges the east/west cultural and political divide that is part of life in the capital city. Its status as a favored venue of musicians speaks volumes about the owners' love of the aural arts and about one neighborhood's support of popular culture.

Friday and Saturday nights produce some of the most music-savvy crowds to be found anywhere in Wisconsin. The fans of the bands are about as multigenerational as one would ever see in a music club, often running from those in their twenties to those in their fifties. It is also fairly common for off-duty musicians to drop in to hear the friendly competition. Some fabled blues legends have passed through these doors. As will some legends in the making.

Longtime tavern hoppers may recall several other interesting bar incarnations on this site. The first version was a post-Prohibition family tavern that drew its customers entirely from a few surrounding residential blocks. In 1944, it was reborn as the Karabis Bar, where mixed crowds of Truax Field airmen and Gisholt machinists could be found with ears glued to wartime radio broadcasts. Big-band sounds and FDR's radio chats probably still rattle around in the pressed-tin ceiling. Later came younger blue-collar crowds, and a jukebox replaced the radio.

Reborn again in 1990 as the Harmony Bar and Grill, the spot had the good fortune to fall into the hands of Keith Daniels and Jo Raggozino. The makeover brought seven tap lines and an ever-changing selection of micro and regional draft beer. Bottled beers and mixed drinks are, of course, available if you can pass up the surprises that greet you nearly every time you look at the tap handles.

Then there's the food. The menu does nothing less than redefine tavern food and, like the rotating beer selections, is a constantly expanding universe. The Italian specialties are very well received by patrons. Many say that this sense of fun and experimentation with the menu accounts for a better following among women than most taverns.

▼ ▼ ▼ ▼ ▼ ▼ ▼ ▼ ▼ ▼ ▼ ▼ ▼ ▼ ▼ ▼ ▼

Warning to cardplayers: you're in sheepshead fanatic territory. The cardplayers are territorial, though nonthreatening, the few jerks in their numbers being far outweighed by a herd of hail-fellows-well-met. It's a gathering place for card-deck devotees so rooted in their affection for the game that they talk of past games as Vikings might recount storied battles. Some of the regulars have even immortalized the games in illustrations and photographs.

▼ ▼ ▼ ▼ ▼ ▼ ▼ ▼ ▼ ▼ ▼ ▼ ▼ ▼ ▼ ▼ ▼ ▼

Madison

Wonders Pub
1980 Atwood Avenue
(608) 244-8563

More than one wag has called Wonders the Pinckney Street Hideaway Revisited after the dearly departed Capitol Square institution. That view does the Atwood Avenue spot a disservice. It's true that Wonders management gained their spurs at Pinckney Street and that many of the core customers migrated to this East Side location. But this is more of a neighborhood bar, doing without the preening of state bureaucrats, the braying of politicians, the smug smirks of lobbyists, and the intrigues of political junkies. Thank goodness!

Wonders also has a more steady day than its deceased downtown stepparent. The flow is consistent into the evening, not just lunchtime and after-work frenzies followed by flight back to the 'burbs. The atmosphere is as laid-back as you'll find in Madison. No trendy crowds looking to see who's looking at them. No gimmicks, no political correctness, and no cliques staking out turf. Just some good beers and decent tavern food and a nice mellow crowd of stand-up folks. It is a fitting stop for out-of-town visitors who want to avoid State Street madness and want something more like home.

A geniune family feeling pervades the regulars in this spot. Quite a few are related by blood or marriage, but even more have the bonds of years of frequenting the same taverns. They just don't drink together, they play together. It's quite common to see groups of Wonders patrons catching a Badger hockey game together or taking in a few innings of minor league baseball with the Madison Black Wolf.

The beer selection does well by Wisconsin specialties. Micros and regionals are in the draft mix, with Guinness for the holdovers from Pinckney Street. More imports are tallied in the bottle coolers. Wonders garners one of the best compliments a tavern can pick up: Stu Becker, former Pinckney Street co-owner, likes to drink here. Good enough for the rest of us.

▼ ▼ ▼ ▼ ▼ ▼ ▼ ▼ ▼ ▼ ▼ ▼ ▼ ▼ ▼ ▼ ▼

Manitowoc
Capone's Pub and Grill
1036 S. 10th Street
(920) 683-8888

Despite a mild gangster motif, there's nothing sinister about this name-sake of the famous Chicago crime boss. Capone's is a favorite with the 30-something crowd, especially at night. The daytime and early-evening crowd is more age diverse, as evidenced by a wide jukebox selection that includes Benny Goodman, Patsy Cline, Jethro Tull, and Blues Traveler.

The 15 taps include Wisconsin's regionals and occasionally an import or two. Capone's switches draft beers to keep up with market developments and consumer preferences. The same sense of experimentation guides their bottled beer selection. At least 25 bottled brews are typically available, including rare finds like Beartooth Blueberry and Riverfest Stein.

Don't be surprised if a Saturday visit puts you in the middle of an informal wedding party. This seems to be the place where young folks go—after the kids and old folks polish off the wedding cake and punch—to loosen ties, take off jackets, and cast aside veils and bouquets. It's a great environment in which to get to know Manitowoc. It's not hard to find someone who will cheerfully give you the who's who of the area and stretch their information back three or four generations. I don't think that Manitowocians are particularly history minded, it's more a matter of the town having so many interwoven family stories. Family still is at the core of life in this fair city, even among these younger folks who frequent Capone's.

With this crowd, you won't hear as many working-class tales of railroading, shipbuilding, and brewing as their fathers and grandfathers might tell. But you will hear a strong work ethic that resonates in a surprising way. I didn't hear any Generation X whining or too-cool cynicism here. Hey, the kids are all right.

Food includes a sandwich menu, appetizers, and salads. Locals seem to favor the Capone Pasta Bowl and the Three Alarm Chili. Yes, it's hot. What's going on in Manitowoc taverns with the incendiary seasonings? Everywhere I went I had people asking me if I needed more hot sauce, more chilis, more salsa, and more horseradish. You can figure on drinking more than one beer to put out the flames.

▼ ▼ ▼ ▼ ▼ ▼ ▼ ▼ ▼ ▼ ▼ ▼ ▼ ▼ ▼ ▼ ▼ ▼

Manitowoc

Hamilton House
1202 10th Street
(920) 683-9331

Abright, cheery neighborhood tavern with one of the most pleasing interiors to be found in a small- to medium-size tavern. Well-placed windows and light colors not only brighten the mood, they show off the Hamilton House's considerably above-average cleanliness. No wonder this downtown spot has many loyal customers among local women.

This is a favorite spot for railroad buffs and travelers on the Lake Michigan car ferry. The owner is a veteran railroad worker. The area's romance with ships, trains, and ships that carry trains is manifest in the art and memorabilia relating to maritime and rail themes. Even better are the legends to be heard when the old-timers start talking about shipwrecks and train derailments. If only I didn't live in the opposite corner of the state, I could sit and listen in for many a rainy day.

Hamilton House is a tavern with a past. Local historical societies have recognized it as a "century tavern" (having started as a tavern over a hundred years ago). It was renowned as the Silver Creek House in the nineteenth century. During Prohibition it fooled federal tax agents with the name "Riederer's Soft Drink Store," even as various alcoholic beverages were manufactured in the cellar. It seems that half of Manitowoc was in on the scam, and the descendants of those who defied this period of despotism still boast of their ancestors' exploits in evading the revenue storm troopers. A careful six-year-long restoration process has preserved the feel of this colorful past.

But don't get me wrong, this is not a hangout for historic preservationists. Beer is spoken here. Eight tap heads assure availability of regional beers on a seasonal basis, with Leinie's Red and Point Bock serving as semipermanent anchors. Fox River and Lakefront microbrews are available in bottles. Regular customers organize a charter bus to brew fests and thus cement their reputation as the truest hopheads in this beer-loving burg.

Hearty eaters recommend the Buffalo Burger. The fish fry is rated above average. But the culinary centerpiece of the Hamilton House is said to be its Friday night lobster bisque. It is so popular that it almost always disappears before 7 P.M. I must confess to stalking the elusive lobster bisque on three separate occasions and coming up empty-handed each time (once at 6:30 P.M. in a blizzard—the place was already packed with warm and smug customers bathed in the perfume of lobster bisque).

▼ ▼ ▼ ▼ ▼ ▼ ▼ ▼ ▼ ▼ ▼ ▼ ▼ ▼ ▼ ▼ ▼

Manitowoc

Linda's Chicago Street Inn
916 Chicago Street
(920) 684-1196

Here's a time machine of a tavern. Step back to the days when blue-collar workers could support their families on one paycheck. A time when a stop for a beer after a shift change was a ritual so widespread that every tavern in Manitowoc was standing room only. A time when news of a factory worker's injury would cause a hat to be passed and a delegation to be sent forthwith to the victim's family. A time when a packed tavern was hushed to silence to hear the call on a Warren Spahn pitch.

Kingsbury, the lakeshore's standard beer of the booming 1950s, still lives on in Manitowoc and has a loyal following at Linda's (even though it has most recently been brewed by G. Heileman in La Crosse). Other than that it has a modest collection of national brews, regionals like Leinenkugel's, and odds and ends like Samuel Adams and Paulaner. But don't suspect for a minute that the modest parameters suggest a lackadaisical attitude toward malt beverages. Like all customer-true taverns, Chicago Street Inn will serve up what its repeat business calls for. Indeed, I found the regulars here more conversant in Wisconsin brewing history and the sweet memories of the tastes of disappeared beers than a roomful of microbrew conventioneers.

It was in this hallowed hall that I first heard the legend of Fritz Kleinnagel. Fritz was the Paul Bunyan of beer drinking, a German-American character woven into the fabric of everything connected to brewing, taverns, and the comaraderie of quaffing beer. Fritz left his tracks up and down the Lake Michigan shoreline from Kenosha to Algoma and west to Lake Winnebago. But Manitowoc was clearly his home base. Local wags suggest that Fritz made sure he left a little bit of himself in Manitowoc by relieving himself in the tanks of the brewery on Marshall Street.

The ambience: friendly bartenders, great old dark-wood back bar, no-frills burgers served on sheets of waxed paper. The crowd: union members, NASCAR racing fans, Vietnam Veterans Motorcycle Club, and some of the crustiest old-timers south of the Yukon (including one raspy Jack Palance look-alike). Don't be thrown off by the fact that many regulars converse at high volume. It's not hostilty, it's hearing loss, and those of us who spent too much of our youth around explosives, revving motors, and industrial machinery fit right in with that part of the crowd. Opens at 6 A.M.!

▼ ▼ ▼ ▼ ▼ ▼ ▼ ▼ ▼ ▼ ▼ ▼ ▼ ▼ ▼ ▼ ▼

Middleton

The Club Tavern
1915 Branch Street
(608) 836-3773

Not a particularly novel name, but descriptive. It is a tavern and night-club and combines those elements well by maintaining two separate bar areas. Makes you wonder when some wag will come up with "Joe's Club Tavern Bar and Grill Lounge-Inn." Name aside, this spot has slowly but surely built up a reputation that reaches far beyond its hometown.

Middleton is known as a sedate bedroom community for Madison, not as a party town. But enter the Club Tavern and you might think you're in downtown La Crosse, or on Milwaukee's Water Street, or grooving on Madison's East Side. Over a period of years, the Club Tavern has managed to accomplish a Madison-area cultural feat: drawing Madison East Siders out of their neighborhoods for a crosstown trip. The music makes this nightspot special: heavy on blues, with dashes of rock and jazz. The live acts keep the joint jumping three and four nights a week. And "home base" status for the Westside Andy/Mel Ford Band pays dividends with a Thursday night blues jam that is more fun than big-name out-of-town acts. Even regulars never tire of that point in the second set when Mel Ford does a number with his guitar behind his back and another where the "licks" are quite literal and his tongue comes into play.

The scene here is a mixture of a number of elements, not the least of which is the warm-weather volleyball league that plays on the deep sand courts just out the back door. On some game nights the volleyball crowd is so numerous as to make it difficult to park nearby, much less get in the door. The games typically end before bands start playing, but there is sometimes a brief overlap during which sweaty coed teams share brewskis with a polo-shirt crowd.

The bands, particularly on jam nights, prompt a good measure of dancing. While the majority of patrons seem to arrive as couples or mixed groups, the regulars are fairly open to dancing with the new arrivals. Based on overheard chatter, it is easy to conclude that potential partners are usually ready, willing, and able to take a turn on the floor. Some of these folks are pretty polished, as I discovered when a woman half my size asked me to dance and proceeded to spin me around without causing grave bodily harm to anyone. Give it a whirl while the old joints can still take the punishment!

Rotated tap selections are very micro- and regional-friendly. Remember, you're just about in hops-smelling distance of the Capital Brewery/Garten Brau facility. The Club Tavern always seems to have the brand-spanking-new seasonal Garten Brau that no one else has on tap. A busy bartender told me they have "30 or 40" bottled beers.

▼ ▼ ▼ ▼ ▼ ▼ ▼ ▼ ▼ ▼ ▼ ▼ ▼ ▼ ▼ ▼ ▼ ▼

Milwaukee

Buck Bradley's Saloon and Eatery
1019 Old World Third Street
(414) 224-8500

"Impressive" is the word most often used by first-time visitors to describe the physical setting at Buck Bradley's. There are three separate bar areas, including a second-floor sports bar. The owners claim that the downstairs bar is the longest bar east of the Mississippi. The boast cannot be substantiated, but it's clear that 50 to 60 people could easily drink along its expanse without too much difficulty. The entire atmosphere is one of spaciousness and comfort.

While you're not likely to run into customers in flannel shirts and earflapped hats, there is a democratic demographic at work here. Conversation with a cross section turned up young steamfitters, middle-aged bankers, a clutch of airline flight attendants, and multigenerational family gatherings. The spot draws pretty evenly from the city, the suburbs, and the downtown convention hotels. Surprising as it may sound in 1999, Buck Bradley's serves as an initiation spot for many folks who are not part of the microbrew and brew pub subculture. So the important role of slaking thirst and whetting curiosity is performed handsomely here.

Buck Bradley's is just a buzzer-shot throw away from the Bradley Center. Staff and management prepare for event nights as if for a friendly invasion, with a special light meal and appetizer menu for the big crowds. But truth be known, crowds can be sizable on routine weekend nights. As noted already, the customers are diverse. They are also in fine form when downtown events are cooking. No problem here when it comes to eliciting a review on a nearby live concert or reliving a basketball game play-by-play.

You can find more extensive beer lists in Milwaukee. Restaurant critics cite other spots for steaks. And a number of traditional music venues might shine brighter in the entertainment department (though don't underestimate Buck Bradley's; some class local contemporary acts hold forth here on occasion). But more than one young couple told me this was their favorite spot for an evening out after a game. It's easy to see that Buck Bradley's combines many elements with flair and aplomb. Those who desire amenities with their brew won't be disappointed.

▼ ▼ ▼ ▼ ▼ ▼ ▼ ▼ ▼ ▼ ▼ ▼ ▼ ▼ ▼ ▼ ▼ ▼ ▼

Milwaukee

Foundation
2718 Bremen Street
(414) 374-2587

It doesn't get much quirkier than the Foundation Skateboard Graveyard and Beer Bar. This neighborhood tavern is home to a unique skateboard collection. Never fear, youngsters in baggy clothes do not wheel down the bar. But you can expect to run into a party here that may include some colorful people or some entourage that just blew in from points unknown. Or you just might hit a time when Milwaukee's guerrilla home brewers are hosting a tasting party. Foundation is also a hangout for a number of musicians and band hangers-on. At least one Milwaukee source (the *Shepherd Express*) gave the bar's jukebox the top rating in the Milwaukee area.

And talk about characters! Each story that filters back to me about this place is stranger than the last. My own foray exposed me to a couple who spoke to each other in dialogue lines lifted from *The Rocky Horror Picture Show*, a juggler with about a dozen body piercings, and a woman who told me she was practicing to be a female impersonator. Were they pulling my leg or other body parts? All I know is that I came away feeling like it was audience participation night at a punk version of public radio's *Hotel Milwaukee* show. But the strangest thing of all is that everyone was as nice as at a small-town homecoming.

Tavern owners seldom recognize how important it is for the establishment to have a personality. It doesn't matter if the ambience is mounted mythological beasts or vehicle license plates. We need more bars with distinctive character. So hats off to this one!

Foundation usually offers eight to ten tap beers. Local brews are well represented, including Sprecher and Lakefront products. The lines from Gray's and New Glarus also have avid followers here. This is not a snooty microbrew bar. It is not embarrassed by its sales volume of Blatz or its unpretentious setting. At Foundation they keep one foot firmly planted in Milwaukee's 1950s tavern tradition and one foot stepping boldly into the twenty-first century. They pull it off.

See if you can play the skateboard video game better than I did. It's as different as everything else in this distinctly offbeat but upbeat place.

▼ ▼ ▼ ▼ ▼ ▼ ▼ ▼ ▼ ▼ ▼ ▼ ▼ ▼ ▼ ▼ ▼ ▼

Milwaukee
Hampton House
5403 West Hampton Avenue
(414) 461-2108

A neighborhood bar is usually the last place you expect to find diversity. In many places, the neighborhood bar is still a reflection of the ethnic identity or socioeconomic class of the predominant group in surrounding residential areas. But here, in one of America's most segregated cities, we have in Hampton House a long-standing tradition of African-American and European-American customer mingling.

The atmosphere is friendly, not forced, and reflects the positive side of social changes in Milwaukee over the last few decades. In some cases the friendships span several generations. Fathers may have worked in the machine shop together and daughters may have attended UW-Milwaukee together. Not surprisingly, it is a comfortable spot for those with multiracial backgrounds. That is a growing portion of the population, and eventually smart businesspeople will figure out it's a niche market.

This establishment carves its own tranquil spot in the complex business of creating community in a diverse environment. Candid talk with customers disabuses one of any utopian fantasies. Different people getting along in the hustle and bustle of competitive urban life will always be a challenge. What is heartening about people I met here is how unassuming and honest they are about their responsibility for building that new world that most of us want.

This is one of the few places in Wisconsin where I have run into people who still talk about the unfinished business of civil rights, not the language of intergroup grievances. If you build some trust in this circle you just might get a person or two to open up about the long, hot summers of the past and the stories and humor of cultural misunderstandings.

Not a micro bar, but there are some hometown and regional beers to be had. The big pastime is dart throwing. The restaurant portion of the business also has a neighborhood following.

▼ ▼ ▼ ▼ ▼ ▼ ▼ ▼ ▼ ▼ ▼ ▼ ▼ ▼ ▼ ▼ ▼

Milwaukee

Landmark 1850 Inn
5905 S. Howell Avenue
(414) 769-1850

Milwaukee's oldest tavern! What more need be said about a history-steeped spot that hosted rebellious Whigs planning the formation of the Republican Party and Free Soil vigilantes fresh off a mission to liberate a fugitive slave? What more could be remarked on this classic building, only two years younger than the state of Wisconsin itself? What further praise could be uttered about its hospitality, which is already lauded to the heights by magazine writers and beer fanciers?

Well, one could say that the Landmark 1850 Inn is in the heart of South Side Milwaukee. One could praise a kitchen open seven evenings a week (this is a nightspot, kitchen hours 3 P.M. to closing). One could give thanks for published coupons conferring complimentary and discounted goodies upon customers. And one could find fellowship with the other patrons of this fair inn.

The spot does draw some history buffs, but I found far more patrons who are quietly making history. The Landmark 1850 Inn seems to be a favorite among those who do their share of downtown lunches and have their fill of being seen at same. The folks I run into are usually involved with business associations, nonprofit organizations, educational groups, and fraternal orders. So I get the sense that a fair amount of networking goes on here.

It also seems to be a place where people open up about what makes Milwaukee tick. This city of beer and sausage is not a terribly introspective place, and it is often hard to get answers about the inner workings of civic life. Sometimes it seems like the formal structure of the community is just an illusion and the real shots are being called elsewhere. The patrons at the Landmark 1850 Inn have often shared astute observations with me about the intrigues surrounding Milwaukee's world of finance and development. Oddly enough, many of the tales lead back to the great brewing fortunes. You can get lost in those plotlines.

But don't forget the beer. A "suds club" here honors those stout hearts who have partaken of 49 draft brews. Those sturdy souls thereafter get to down their beverage of choice in liter mugs. Sample the rare draft treats: Lindeman's Belgium Fromboise, La Trappe Trappist Ale, New Glarus Apple Ale, Hofbrau Oktoberfest, and Paulaner Dunkel Weiss among them. Yum!

▼ ▼ ▼ ▼ ▼ ▼ ▼ ▼ ▼ ▼ ▼ ▼ ▼ ▼ ▼ ▼ ▼

Milwaukee
Landmark Lanes
2220 N. Farwell Avenue
(414) 278-8770

L andmark Lanes has been sniped at in Milwaukee's newspapers and magazines as the place to go for a walk on the dark side. The place is panned by
suburban entertainment writers for its funky crowd and late-night drink
specials ($4 pitchers, $1.75 import bottles, and $1.50 pints, 9 P.M. to bar time).
But those folks like the bright lights. Have they no appreciation for the real
heartbeat of the city?

It's true Landmark Lanes has a notes-from-the-underground feel. But many
of us interpret its atmosphere as a deft combination of bowling alley and un-
dercover agent rendezvous site. More than a few public defenders, detectives,
and investigative writers have mentioned this spot as a place where information
can be found and the tip of the unseen Milwaukee can be glimpsed. Folklore
has it that the principals of a famous espionage case dallied here and that labor
union and political power struggles have been settled here by incognito insid-
ers. Never fear, intrigue does not translate into sinister surroundings—the spot
is safe if you apply urban common sense.

Some of my favorite Milwaukee barroom buds like to hang out here. They're
honest about liking the atmosphere as much as the beer. It is a place where stories can run as light and cheery as a fine pilsner or as dark and heavy as a coffee
stout. Many of my favorite tale spinners in this joint come down somewhere
between the conflicted tales of morally ambiguous postindustrial life and the
blunt sensationalism of true-crime tabloids. On the other hand, I know of no
other place in Milwaukee where a ribald story resonates quite so well. All
through the various narrations there is the endless sipping.

How about that beer? First-time visitors are surprised to find 39 tap lines
and 75 types of bottled beer. The selections balance the giants, the micros, the
regionals, and the imports. Put on your trenchcoat or leather jacket and don
your sunglasses.

▼ ▼ ▼ ▼ ▼ ▼ ▼ ▼ ▼ ▼ ▼ ▼ ▼ ▼ ▼ ▼ ▼ ▼

Milwaukee

La Perla
734 S. Fifth Street
(414) 645-9888

A Friday night hotspot in a noted Mexican-American restaurant on Milwaukee's South Side. The lively crowd mixes plenty of Spanish and Spanish accents with German-American and Polish-American customers. The mood is more samba and Latin disco than mariachi. As one regular put it, "It's a good place to go if you can't get away to Puerto Vallarta." To that claim my response is it's better in food and hospitality, lacking only the warm and sunny weather that drives one south of the border in winter.

La Perla serves the full range of tropical drinks, with blender concoctions being very popular. If there's a bigger tequila selection in Wisconsin, I haven't seen it. The primary Mexican beers are available (Modela, Negra Modelo, Carta Blanca, Pacifico, Dos Equis, Dos Equis Lager Bohemia, and Corona) along with other domestics and imports. No simple cantina, La Perla's bar is among the classiest spots in Milwaukee to imbibe your favorite beverage.

All 50-plus restaurant menu items can be ordered in the bar. It's clear that many of the regular customers routinely take their meals in the bar. The *botanas* (appetizers) and combination plates seem to be the main barroom fare. But as I sipped my Dos Equis and nibbled fresh tortilla chips on my first visit, the businessman on the next stool went to work on sautéed lobster and garlic sauce.

This bright, well-lit restaurant has secure parking, which is reassuring to out-of-towners after they approach through a dimly lit warehouse district. The outside patio area is a slice of Margaritaville in summer. In the winter the deck is covered with a walled-in tent, warmed by kerosene heaters and filled with tables. This may sound a little like field manuevers with NATO or mess hall à la *M*A*S*H*, but it's quite cozy and altogether serviceable. Not to mention that it keeps down the waiting time to be seated. So bravo to La Perla management. Check out the collection of hundreds of hot sauces in the bar.

▼ ▼ ▼ ▼ ▼ ▼ ▼ ▼ ▼ ▼ ▼ ▼ ▼ ▼ ▼ ▼

Milwaukee
Milwaukee Ale House
233 N. Water Street
(414) 226-2337
www.ale-house.com

One of Wisconsin's most acclaimed brew pubs, the Milwaukee Ale House is a hangout for those connected to the microbrewing industry. The person next to you at the bar might be a microbrewery owner, a sales rep from a malt processor, or a brewery equipment engineer. But your stoolmate could just as well turn out to be "Joe from da South Side." And who can blame him for wandering into the land of "da suits." The beer and the food stand out even in a town with no shortage of choices.

Yes, the beer! Let me count the ways. For the novice palate, there is the honey wheat Downtown Lites. For the hardy veteran, there is Sheepshead Stout, brimming with the rich taste of dark-roasted malt. In between are the full-bodied Session Ale, the specialty-hopped Pull Chain Pale Ale, the golden Solomon Juneau Ale, and the smooth-malted Louie's Demise Ale. All distinctive and worth sampling before you zero in on a favorite.

The Ale House was in the process of experimenting with its menu when I visited it for this guide. If the "test" of Creole sausage and gumbo are any indication, there is expert work going on in the kitchen. Feedback from my Milwaukee sources continues to be extremely positive.

The management has wisely avoided the chauvinism that overtakes many full-line brew pubs. They are confident enough about their products (and yet solicitous of customer preferences) to offer many other Wisconsin microbrews. Among the initial offerings: Lakefront Pumpkin, Capital Octoberfest, Wisconsin Badger Porter, Sprecher Brown Pub Ale, and Fox River Caber Tossing Scottish Ale. They expect to offer seasonal brews from most of Wisconsin's microbreweries. Few establishments get off to such an auspicious start.

As if all this wasn't enough, the Ale House is building an impressive wine list, a decent selection of scotch, and a trove of fine cigars. Live music almost every night! Here I arrive at a strange complaint. The Ale House books some wonderful acts that would have people up on their feet in most other places, but not here. Sure, the dance area is the size of a postage stamp. But a word of advice to you too-cool types who don't like to perspire in your tailored shirts: loosen your ties and lighten up.

▼ ▼ ▼ ▼ ▼ ▼ ▼ ▼ ▼ ▼ ▼ ▼ ▼ ▼ ▼ ▼ ▼

Milwaukee

O'Brien's Sports Bar and Grill
N. 49th and W. Vliet Streets
(414) 453-6200

Many tavern denizens (myself included) dread change, especially when they've grown accustomed to the comfort and amenities of a time-worn watering hole. This was once the site of a novel import-beer tavern called the Golden Zither. But that was many bottles ago, and in this case the past is redeemed and expanded upon. My brew scouts give the new place a hearty thumbs-up and commend the updated offerings and look.

O'Brien's logs in with 17 beer taps. The microbrew mainstays are the local products from Lakefront and Sprecher. The import side of the ledger tilts toward the British Isles with Newcastle, Harp, and Guinness. They plan to carry a bottle inventory of around a hundred brands. Look for $2 import night on Thursdays.

The crowd is lively and beer focused, though you find less of the beer-sampling crowd here and more customers who know what they like. The mood is decidedly different than in the downtown establishments—more of a sense of dropping by for a fitting end to the day rather than knocking back a quick drink before scooting out to the 'burbs. The neighborhood has undergone some changes but is still remembered by most as the core of Milwaukee's solid working-class families. It's kind of interesting when those who've hung on in these parts encounter the self-styled urban renewalists who are now coming back from the 'burbs. Provides some good material for the amateur sociologists among us.

Music is building up a following, too. The plan is to have regular nights for blues, rock, jazz, and Irish bands. The menu is expanding from sandwiches into fish fry territory and pizza. Plans for an outside beer garden are in the works. This bar is one that I expect to chart to see if it lives up to its potential.

▼ ▼ ▼ ▼ ▼ ▼ ▼ ▼ ▼ ▼ ▼ ▼ ▼ ▼ ▼ ▼ ▼

Milwaukee
Turner Restaurant Bar
1034 N. Fourth Street
(414) 276-4844

No tour of Wisconsin's imbibing establishments would be complete without mention of the bar in the Historic Turner Restaurant (yes, the word "historic" is part of the formal business name). The landmark building is deeply steeped in the cultural and political traditions of Wisconsin's German community. Turner *Verein*, or clubs, once dotted the landscape and served as athletic clubs for Wisconsin's largest ethnic group. The Milwaukee association kept this building in good repair and offered good food and drink to five generations of German Americans.

Perhaps more importantly, the continuation of the Turner club established a link with Milwaukee's golden age. It was a time not of an ethnic minority in an American city, but of a German city in the American heartland. This meant lectures, concerts, choral societies, newspapers, publishing houses, and all manner of learned professions carried out within a central European worldview. The leisurely Sunday spent in parks with the family and a bucket of beer was no small part of this milieu and accounted for the bitter resistance in Milwaukee toward the Prohibition movement. Turner Hall is seen by many as a monument to those times.

Then came the renovations of the last decade. Many of the regulars think the changes swept away the worn beer hall charm that provided their Friday night sanctuary. But the murals, artifacts, and photograph collection remain. So do the traditional elements of the menu. If anything, the fish fry and sandwiches are better than ever. Indeed, many younger folks are returning to the place Grandpa took them to years ago. It is a great piece in the downtown refurbishing puzzle.

As for the beer, there is a growing emphasis on the local microbrews, and the import collection is up to about two dozen Teutonic favorites. The bar setting is virtually a gilded palace. Besides the bar and an elegant dining area, there are also party and meeting rooms that are suitable for large group entertaining.

▼ ▼ ▼ ▼ ▼ ▼ ▼ ▼ ▼ ▼ ▼ ▼ ▼ ▼ ▼ ▼ ▼ ▼

Milwaukee

Water Street Brewery
1101 N. Water Street
(414) 272-1195
www.restaurantour.com/wsb

B ack in 1987 it seemed a bold proposition to combine a small brewery and a restaurant. Since then such combos are springing up all over the place. But despite many excellent additions to the downtown Milwaukee scene, loyal patrons cast their votes for this trailblazer. Water Street shows no sign of letting up or running out of steam.

It would be difficult to catalog the range of brews to come out of Water Street kettles over the years. Never averse to experimentation, they still punch out novel seasonal beers in addition to six house brews that do justice to the usual brew pub light to dark range. The experimentation throws off some consumers. But many true hopheads appreciate the fine-tuning that has gone into Water Street brews over the years. Their efforts have not gone unnoticed in brewing trade publications.

Lunch is offered in the form of appetizers, sandwiches, and salads. A dinner menu comes into play in the evening hours. Self-aware as an "institution," Water Street Brewery offers tours and souvenir sales. Growing numbers of out-of-town visitors are learning that no trip to Milwaukee is complete without a visit to Water Street.

This venerable establishment is physically very similar to the best of Germany's upgraded beer halls: spacious, airy, and bright. There is one main area that is the proverbial three-ring circus but with even more action for the eye. Other smaller spaces serve private groups and overflow. Even the larger hall has a feel of multiple centers of activity, with enough elbow room that sizable gatherings of friends and coworkers can grab a table or two and not impinge on a neighboring group.

As the preceding Milwaukee entries show, there are places aplenty where beer lovers congregate to savor beer, appreciate beer, and even venerate beer. Water Street elicits all those responses and adds a few that it has earned by virtue of its seniority. The one element that it preserves that is often forgotten in the serious brew pub is pure fun. There is more laughter here than in any other similar operation.

It's no accident that the groups that meet to celebrate brewing history, swap home brew recipes, and plan beer festival events often pick Water Street as the place to hatch their plots or kick off their efforts. The atmosphere is contagious. Stop in and kick off a little beer adventure of your own.

▼ ▼ ▼ ▼ ▼ ▼ ▼ ▼ ▼ ▼ ▼ ▼ ▼ ▼ ▼ ▼ ▼

Milwaukee
Zur Krone
839 S. Second St.
(414) 647-1910

Milwaukee's discriminating beer drinkers have heralded Zur Krone since 1976, earning this small but beer-packed spot the "best beer selection" award from the *Shepherd Express* weekly. The bottled selection weighs in at a hefty 300 imports and micros. Twelve taps grace the bar with rare draft gems like Berghoff Hazelnut and Bitburger. Known as the "home of the boot" and "home of the five-liter stein," it draws as savvy a beer-drinking crowd as can be found anywhere. Trendy folks may think they've discovered good beer on spruced-up Water Street, but many tavern pros believe the whole movement toward better beer in Wisconsin started at Zur Krone.

The astute observer can trace the lineage here and reconstruct the steps by which good beer made a comeback in America after the macrobucks macrobreweries waged their brutally successful post–World War II effort to crush local breweries. Take a generation of Cold War GIs garrisoned in Germany, England, and other temperate beer-drinking climes. Add a youth culture of vagabond travel and appreciation of different tastes. Top off with growing consumer demand on all fronts for items that embody quality and authenticity. Conversations with Zur Krone patrons will confirm that all these trends combined to resurrect beer that tastes like beer. Maybe someday this spot will be a shrine.

A limited but tasty menu complements the beer: fish fry, burgers, smoked sausages, bratwurst, liverwurst, and a cheese plate. The CD collection here is an added bonus. Many veterans of Milwaukee's pub crawl army think of Zur Krone as the premier jumping-off or wrap-up spot for their tours. A decent tour can be made right in the neighborhood, with Wilbur's, the Dubliner, and many others close at hand.

It's not surprising that the crowd and the hired help here would know a thing or two about microbrews and imports. But I was taken aback when five customers at the bar reeled off critiques of over 200 Milwaukee-area neighborhood taverns. Talk about sage company. It turned out that they were all off-duty bartenders. You know you're in the right place when it caters to the pros.

▼ ▼ ▼ ▼ ▼ ▼ ▼ ▼ ▼ ▼ ▼ ▼ ▼ ▼ ▼ ▼ ▼ ▼ ▼

ANOTHER ROUND

Some Milwaukee Beer Facts

Beer made Milwaukee famous because of location, resources, and immigration patterns. Milwaukee sat astride the new rail routes. It had ready access to grain for brewing and wood for barrels. The waves of German immigrants brought brewing experience and consumer demand.

Miller's flagship brew, High Life, was named in a 1906 contest. The logo for many years was the "Girl in the Moon," who in various depictions wore a witchlike hat and wielded a whip. Miller diverted its production during World War II to our troops overseas and built up a national following.

Pabst Brewing Company was one of the first breweries to understand the marketing potential of awards. It actively promoted the beer at nineteenth-century fairs and expositions. Pabst beer garnered honors at the 1876 Philadelphia Centennial Exposition, the 1878 Paris World's Fair, and the 1893 Columbia Exposition in Chicago. In 1892 the company used 300,000 yards of blue ribbon, a snip of which was wrapped around the neck of each bottle of its premium beer. After World War II, Pabst evolved into a working-class favorite. By the 1990s closure of the Milwaukee facilities and cuts in benefits for retired brewery workers had made the name a dirty word in union halls.

▼ ▼ ▼ ▼ ▼ ▼ ▼ ▼ ▼ ▼ ▼ ▼ ▼ ▼ ▼ ▼ ▼

Oshkosh

Oblio's
434 Main Street
(920) 426-1063

Good beer is not a recent fad at Oblio's. The tradition is inching up on 20 years of quality domestic and international selections. Some would say that the good folks here are just hitting their stride. The tap lineup boasts 26 micros, imports, regionals, and giant industrial brews. The bottled collection tallies about 35 types.

Beverage selection doesn't stop at malt and hop juice; the martini menu is a draw for some of the after-work crowd. Also worthy of note are 10 single-malt scotches. This downtown spot is a great alternative to the prefab pubs springing up out on the fringe at malls. The light-wood interior gives it a Northwoods resort feel and makes a stop here feel like a minivacation. Oblio's is the spot to which brew fans head after the annual Oshkosh Blues 'n Brews Festival. And why not? The spot has probably done more to educate beer palates on the west side of Lake Winnebago than any other business in the Fox Valley.

It's also a good place to get the lowdown on other goings-on in the Fox Valley. My conversations here usually are enhanced by customers who are in the know about the local arts and culture scene, such as events on area campuses and fund-raisers for local civic groups. It's definitely a wired-in crowd.

On the other hand, there is some representation within Oblio's corps of regulars from the lake sports enthusiasts. That means almost everything from soup to nuts that would occur out on big Lake Winnebago. But mostly it means boaters, who fall into three categories. There are the big-boat fans of partying on the water. Then there are those who love their watercraft small, fast, and sporty. Lastly, you'll find some of the sailing crowd. OK, a windsurfer or two might drop by.

▼ ▼ ▼ ▼ ▼ ▼ ▼ ▼ ▼ ▼ ▼ ▼ ▼ ▼ ▼ ▼ ▼ ▼

Oshkosh

Packers Pub
1603 West 20th Avenue
(920) 231-3517

Guess what interest tops the list at this spot? Actually, gridiron passion is only part of the story. While Packer hearts may beat beneath their green and gold attire, patrons here make the place lively throughout all four seasons. Next door is La Sures Cafe and Catering, and together the two businesses make this stretch of 20th Avenue just about the busiest block in Winnebago County on Friday night. Packers Pub is proof that the bustle of the neighborhood tavern can be carried out to the edge of a city as it changes through growth. The trick is meshing with the new patterns of housing and business development and, unfortunately, conceding that almost all patrons will arrive by car. That slam at Fox Valley land use aside, Packers Pub does the after-work tavern tradition proud.

Speaking of Friday night, arrive before the after-work crowd starts filing in—it often ends up four deep at the bar. So what's the draw? The menu is not extensive, though they make a darn good chicken salad sandwich. The average customer might think of Coors as a premium beer, but press a bit and they'll admit they've heard of Leinenkugel.

It probably comes down to nice people having a good time in a comfortable setting. There's a fairly even gender distribution here among this sports-inclined, but not couch potato, crowd. These are not just spectators—there are plenty of golfers, softball players, and winter-sports enthusiasts here, both male and female.

Packers Pub runs on a seasonal cycle not too different from that of many Wisconsin taverns: football season at the center, various sports playoffs following, and the rear brought up by a variety of special events in the family calendar like anniversaries, birthdays, and graduations. If you happen to be in the area on a Packer road game day, this is definitely the place to watch the game.

Another interesting local phenomenon occurs during the summer when the annual aviation event hits town. All manner of pilots, jet junkies, military aircraft buffs, and aerospace business types descend on Oshkosh and take this and virtually every other bar over for the duration. It's a great time if you like aircraft and don't mind humongous crowds. I sat in Packers Pub on one occasion and heard crop dusters, stunt pilots, and airline executives trade insults with World War II bomber pilots. I'll always remember Packers Pub as the place where I finally met the Navy pilot who nearly bombed me in Vietnam 30 years ago. Apology and round of beer accepted.

▼ ▼ ▼ ▼ ▼ ▼ ▼ ▼ ▼ ▼ ▼ ▼ ▼ ▼ ▼ ▼ ▼

Poynette

Hookers Resort
Highway V at Lake Wisconsin
(608) 635-7867

Hookers has earned the loyalty of three and four generations within the families that frequent the east bank of the Lake Wisconsin section of the Wisconsin River. Even those who didn't spend their childhoods here will feel the connection to those family-friendly lakeside taverns of 40 and 50 years ago. These are very precious pieces of the cultural landscape and are threatened by trends in the use of shoreline property that act to price small businesses out of such spots and give them over to playgrounds and retreats for the well-off. It's a touchy matter that agitates the nerves connected to our populist sensibilities and to our conservationist values.

Older patrons can fill you in about their memories of polkas and square dances. There was a time when the Poynette radio station would plug the performances by having the musicians give live on-air samples. Many a big name passed through Columbia County courtesy of this process. These days the bands present contemporary country and oldies rock on Friday and Saturday nights. Wednesdays bring line dancing and Sundays often bring jam sessions. Schedules can vary due to reserved evenings for wedding parties and reunions, so call ahead.

The bar is not fancy but has a loyal following. The 30 bottled brews do not include many exotics, being anchored chiefly by the big guys in Milwaukee and St. Louis. However, effort is made to keep the complete Leinie's craft line on hand. Morning-after visitors will also appreciate the good-sized Bloody Mary served with full-size pickle and beefstick.

The Hookers bar menu is limited to sandwiches and deep-fried appetizers. If you saunter over to the dining room you can rustle up steaks and fish, including perch, cod, walleye, and the rarely seen bluegill. The resort side of the business is a bit of "up north" without the long drive. Cabins are available. Good fishing can be found on the river and at nearby Columbia Lake. The adjacent marina provides canoe rentals, excursions, and return transport.

If you're up for conversation at Hookers, catch a Saturday afternoon crowd on a winter day after a cold spell that has created mass cabin fever. This is when the area's true brandy sippers crawl out to see their shadows and limber up their tales of ice fishing, snow softball, snow golf, and the gentlemen's ice sport of curling. Or show up some Friday night near the time of the summer solstice, when the purple rays of the fading sunset darn near bump up against evening news time. These are the dog days of fishermen's lies, comic boat mishaps, and encounters with DNR conservation wardens. Either way you're likely to run into a Gunderson who'll work in a Norwegian joke.

39

▼ ▼ ▼ ▼ ▼ ▼ ▼ ▼ ▼ ▼ ▼ ▼ ▼ ▼ ▼ ▼ ▼ ▼ ▼

Racine

Swingers
2322 Lathrop Avenue
(262) 554-0880

A visit to Swingers is not a visit to the Racine that many of us knew in the days of bustling machine shops and heavy equipment manufacturing. It is becoming harder and harder to find traces of that Racine. In a sense, a spot like Swingers is emblematic of the shift in economic base that many of Wisconsin's midrange cities were forced to muddle through. Though one can hear nostalgic laments for many lost shot-and-a-beer joints, there is a clear understanding that the customer base has changed and that many of the enduring bars now offer more customer options.

The six-tap rotation at Swingers is usually anchored by Hacker-Pschorr and Rolling Rock, with guest appearances by Sprecher and Gray's products. The bottled list tallies around 25 to 30 brands from among the big-name imports, domestic nationals, and a few micros. Inexplicably, pumpkin ale has followers here beyond the seasonal demand at Halloween and Thanksgiving. Many regulars come for the daily drink specials, and many women customers like the hot nut-honey drink.

Swingers adopts that all-things-to-all-people approach taken by T.G.I. Friday's and other chains. That's not a put-down; it's good to see an independent adapt to wide-band consumer demand. One senses that the appeal here represents a generational changing of the tavern guard. The old after-work tavern was often a totally male domain. In those days, when a man went out with the wife for a drink in Racine, he put on a coat and a tie. Nowadays, the prime age base of taverngoers in places like Racine is looking for a middle ground, and Swingers provides it. The atmosphere is casual but the food is many notches above that.

One of my favorite things about the crowd at Swingers is that they're young enough to move on to the next phase of tavern life, but old enough to have an appreciation for what has been lost in the neighborhoods of Racine and places like Kenosha, Cudahy, South Milwaukee, and West Allis. A few even played a little game of Dad's/Granddad's favorite bar. The way I heard it during my visit, this trivial but nostalgic pursuit was consciously part homage and part send-up. How else can you explain the sentimental tears shed at the loss of the forebears' manly haunts along with the guffaws over the urinals that backed up during the celebrations marking the end of World War II and stayed clogged until the day the business died?

▼ ▼ ▼ ▼ ▼ ▼ ▼ ▼ ▼ ▼ ▼ ▼ ▼ ▼ ▼ ▼ ▼ ▼

Racine

Yardarm Bar and Grill
930 Erie Street
(262) 633-8270

The nautical crew ties up here in weather fair and foul. The atmosphere is, naturally, driven by the maritime theme and includes artifacts from vessels such as Aristotle Onassis's mega yacht and Lake Michigan shipwrecks. But don't expect boating snobbery here—the putt-putt skiff folks mingle with the nattily attired sailing crowd. In addition, plenty of landlubbers come on board just because a friend told them the place is seaworthy.

The Yardarm sails with ten taps of rotating selections but is often graced with the likes of Guinness, Bass, Harp, Newcastle, Rolling Rock, and Leinenkugel. The bottled selection of 20 beers runs more toward the big nationals, though Illinois boaters have created a demand for Goose Island microbrews. The two-for-one Bloody Mary special has a following among regular patrons. Crowd profile tilts quite a bit toward groups, small and large, who arrive together. But that should not deter the lone castaway from seeking refuge on these shores.

The sandwiches and seafood have a good reputation. The grilled sea bass is spoken of fondly. The Yardarm burger was, in recent memory, cited as a Wisconsin standout. Live music finds its way here on a fairly regular basis (more in summer). It's the type of place with a lot of comings and goings of transient customers. That sort of position often makes it difficult for an establishment to develop a core of regulars who are the necessary ingredient in incubating a tavern culture. But the Yardarm does indeed have its loyal locals and its repeat out-of-towners who crew the place on a sustained basis and keep it shipshape for the new passengers.

Don't expect the type of maritime conversation that you might find in Algoma, Manitowoc, or Superior. You won't find leather-skinned freighter hands in here. But you will find spillover from Racine's summertime lake events, be they sailing or fishing tournaments. Just as likely is an encounter with the movers and shakers of Racine and a dialogue on the changes that first rocked the city and then brought it back. On occasion the talk turns to the Old World Racine, which, while not as thoroughly European as Milwaukee in its heyday, had pockets of Continental charm that still echo today. A little prodding will help the locals wax eloquent on their kringle pastries from Denmark, the kitchen practices from Italy, and the fish dishes from Norway. Try as the developers might to reinvent things, this is still Wisconsin.

Sheboygan

Dave's Who's Inn
835 Indiana Avenue
(920) 457-9832

Weekend nights may test your eardrums with heavy metal music. But, as they say, if it's too loud, you're too old for these nights (unless your favorite bands of the sixties and seventies already left you hearing impaired). Luckily the high-volume stuff is upstairs and the drinks are cheaper on the ground floor. But don't discount the possibility that you might just have some interesting exchanges with the regulars. You just need to yell a little louder.

Some observers see Dave's as the best young blue-collar bar between Milwaukee and Green Bay. The label is a bit deceptive since you're likely to see some gray beards come in for the food and game area. It has its own following for its Friday night perch plate, and broasted chicken is served throughout the week. It's this crowd that has the widest range and the most offbeat characters. But they like to chow down together. Regulars say it's the best place in town for a pickup game of darts or pool (four tables).

Dave's is also home to an odd custom of washing down chicken wings with large quantities of Foster's draft lager. The Australian brew is used as a chaser for regular, hot, or nuclear versions of the poultry appendage. No one could tell me how the tradition started, and as far as anyone knew there was no local link to Down Under.

My roving band of merry men did find a traveling subculture here that has made forays as far as Sun Prairie, if not Sydney. Some of the young fellows who frequent this spot work in construction and installation trades. We heard about road building, electronic cable laying, and pipeline construction. So our group of middle-aged guys received a lesson in where the metal crowd hangs out these days, where the hot after-hours raves go down, and where young laborers get their tattoos. We also found a tradition among some of Dave's patrons that involves celebration of seasonal layoffs and departure for sunnier climes. This is a new spin to the old building trades custom of using winter for hunting, ice fishing, and tavern hopping. Come that January subzero blast, you can't blame them.

▼ ▼ ▼ ▼ ▼ ▼ ▼ ▼ ▼ ▼ ▼ ▼ ▼ ▼ ▼ ▼ ▼ ▼

Sheboygan
Zieggy's Bar and Grill
933 Indiana Avenue
(920) 457-3325

F amily-style taverns have fallen somewhat out of style as soccer moms and dads must spend more time chauffeuring Ryan and Brittany to activities and less time socializing with aunts, uncles, and neighbors. In Sheboygan, the tradition is kept alive with Zieggy's Saturday-afternoon brat fries, junior brass bands, and dart tournaments. The result is a cordial tavern where advice, directions, and gossip are readily dispensed along with the beer.

It also acts as a statement that this straight-arrow portion of the Sheboyganese, exemplary work habits aside, understand the need to slow down the pace. It is unusual to find a cluster of folks like this who openly repudiate the money chase in favor of spending time with family and friends. One old sage remarked that the hurried pace of life these days has done more to harm tavern fellowship than drinking age changes, traffic safety concerns, and competing entertainment options. The end of the workday once offered the promise of unwinding time. Now it's errand time. Zieggy's seems to understand that and fights against the trend.

Zieggy's is a no-frills, country tavern in the city. Patrons come back often for chicken-to-go orders, and the practice is catching on with travelers and fishing parties. Loyalists claim this home turf as the lakeshore's most rabid Packerbacker bar. There are those from Port Washington to Two Rivers who would dispute that, but this crowd is definitely in the running. What is beyond dispute is the sociable nature of the people on both sides of the bar. A vehicle problem in our party of pub pilgrims was met by a four-person volunteer crew out of Zieggy's, including one who went home for tools to effect the needed repair.

The Good Samaritan episode presented another rare slice of life when one up-in-years sidewalk supervisor came out to educate us about road etiquette in the Depression era. He related some interesting stories about a code of the road that evolved as more people had access to automobiles and roved the newly paved highways. He made it sound like every breakdown was a social occasion as other motorists stopped to assist and nearby farmers brought out cool water. And he claimed, with a wink of the eye, that the helpee owed the helpers a drink the next time they met in a tavern. Never let it be said that we didn't repay our obligation.

The beer selection is not extensive, but it does include bottled Point and Leinie's. We cheerfully bought a half dozen Points for our volunteer mechanics. Anheuser-Busch craft brews are available on tap, and they were still in fine form during our visit. Private parties often fill the dining area, so you can expect to have your perch sandwich and beer at the bar with the regulars.

▼ ▼ ▼ ▼ ▼ ▼ ▼ ▼ ▼ ▼ ▼ ▼ ▼ ▼ ▼ ▼ ▼ ▼ ▼

ANOTHER ROUND

What's In a Tavern Name?

Many tavern owners consider the naming process one of the most important steps in starting a business. The names they choose often fuse personal identity with the business identity. Sometimes the names project an image that builds a community and attracts a desired clientele.

Tavern names run from distinguished to mundane to madcap. Among Wisconsin's 14,000-plus taverns are both diversity and recurrent themes. One-of-a-kind names are balanced by a handful of names that are repeated over and over upon the landscape.

The moniker "Sportsmen's Bar," and its variants, wins the prize for sheer numbers. You can't drive far without seeing the name. Indeed, Scott Stenger of Wisconsin's Tavern League told me that many people play a pub crawling game that credits those who find the first Sportsmen's and the most Sportsmen's.

There are numerous "Anchor Inns"—some far from water. Tavern owners make liberal use of the handle "Fireside," notwithstanding the lack of fireplaces or woodstoves. Many others incorporate their highway number in the name, as in Club 117.

On the other hand, Wisconsin taverns also sport names that reflect whimsy, cynicism, insider humor, and long nights of cheap liquor. Some record our heritage and serve as cultural benchmarks. A handful even reflect modern culture's marital instability with X'd-out spouse names still visible on signs.

Pardtown Pub of Linden is a favorite in the heritage category. The name records the original name and ambience of this 1827 Cornish settlement. The Grey Ghost of Forest Junction has a name that echoes.

My list of fun names includes: The Place To Be (Appleton), Dusty's Full Time Country Saloon (Menasha), ICU [Intensive Care Unit] Lounge (Neenah), Someplace (Eagle), Slip-Er-In (Delafield), The Recovery Room (La Crosse), Sit'N Bull (Cataract), Lizard Lounge (Oshkosh), Twisted Sisters (Sobieski), and Emotional Rescue (Beaver Dam). But the absolute winner has to be Louie's Godzilla Lounge and Ancient Chinese Tavern in Milwaukee.

▼ ▼ ▼ ▼ ▼ ▼ ▼ ▼ ▼ ▼ ▼ ▼ ▼ ▼ ▼ ▼ ▼

Shorewood
Village Pub
4488 N. Oakland Avenue
(414) 961-9879

This north shore spot has built up a solid reputation for quality scotch, bourbon, and cigars (if the names Arturo Fuente, Macanudo, and Don Tomas don't mean anything to you, well, it's not 50-cent stogie country). But many have overlooked the respectable beer collection of over 100 micros and imports. The micros do well by Wisconsin's fledgling breweries, and the imports represent a busman's holiday of Germany, the Netherlands, Belgium, and the British Isles.

Wall murals depicting Wisconsin history provide a backdrop for the sports crowd often gathered around five TV screens. The fans and patrons are well informed about sports and follow their teams closely. While the crowd is heavily Shorewood-based, customers from the west and north 'burbs also drop in. Many appreciate the Village Pub's policy of carryouts until midnight.

Our beer and hospitality survey crew found the place a real gem for its location. We started with an impression that everything in Shorewood had to be snooty and stuffy. Well, you don't have to go far to find places like that. The Village Pub may be the exception that proves the rule. Maybe not. In this refuge we met people who were modest and unassuming in spite of their resources and credentials. One of my bolder companions suggested that these customers were really just the domestics for the upscale crowd that lives in Shorewood.

That assertion was countered by a long and convoluted tale by a Village Pub patron who perversely defended his honor by claiming he had married into money. He went on to tell us a chilling story of loveless marriage to a heartless crone and the endless demands placed upon him. We almost asked him to run away with us. Turned out he was totally pulling our legs; his companions identified him as a dirt-poor Appalachian boy who made his own fortune and had a wife half his age. So methinks "gotcha" is a game known in this spot.

▼ ▼ ▼ ▼ ▼ ▼ ▼ ▼ ▼ ▼ ▼ ▼ ▼ ▼ ▼ ▼ ▼ ▼

Stonebank

Stone Bank Pub and Eatery

N67 W33395 Highway K
(262) 966-1975

Milwaukeeans sneak away to this hidden gem in the far reaches of Waukesha County and try to keep it a secret. The subterfuge has not worked well; those pesky brewing trade rags blew the cover. Still, it is a bit of a task to reach. Many reach it via Highway 16 west of Hartford and thence to Highway C north along Okauchee Lake until you reach Highway K. And a nice drive it is for the city-weary.

Its reputation is built on the 15 imports on tap, with good German representation. The moderate-size bottled collection also catches many recognizable imports and micros. Its repeat customers include quite a few folks who like to rotate their way through the selections (people after my own heart). Regulars believe that this pub is a good place for cocktails, too.

The social scene at the Stone Bank is dominated by the "Thursday Night Stomp," an eclectic mix of solo musicians and small bands. The big event of the year is the September Import and Micro Fest. If you're a micro fan, this is a prime place to meet old buddies and make new ones. The attendees are primarily Milwaukee metro, but the word is getting out in Madison and the Fox Valley. It's more intimate than the regional fests and makes a nice combo with a recreational overnight trip.

Speaking of which, the Stone Bank is strategically sited for those who wish to explore both the northern and southern units of Kettle Moraine. Thus the Stone Bank is beginning to see hikers, trail bikers, and nature gazers of various stripes. Find a good B&B in the area (I'll bet the tavern keepers can steer you to one) and you're set for day trips to Old World Wisconsin, Aztalan, Horicon, and the Hoard dairy museum. Or you can follow the antiques-and-collectibles circuit like some of the couples I encountered here.

One group relished their beers and their accounts of several days of flea markets, shops, and estate auctions. One beer evoked the tale of the group members unknowingly bidding against each other. The second beer spawned the narrative of misreading the antiques price guide and discovering that they had paid a price befitting the original instead of the replica now in their possession. But the third beer lubricated the mellow satisfaction of finding a long-lost treasure.

▼ ▼ ▼ ▼ ▼ ▼ ▼ ▼ ▼ ▼ ▼ ▼ ▼ ▼ ▼ ▼ ▼ ▼

Verona

Riley Tavern
8205 Riley Road
(just off Highway J and Military Ridge Trail)
(608) 845-9150

Don't let the address fool you. This is perhaps Dane County's most revered rural tavern, and it has not yet been overtaken by the sprawl and trophy houses that plague the area. The Riley Tavern long served neighboring farmers and the stray hunter or two. But the Military Ridge Trail brought new customers in bicyclist garb.

From the beer drinkers' perspective, the Riley Tavern is a welcome departure from the country bar surrender to Coors and Budweiser. Here we have a respectable sampler of southcentral Wisconsin beer: Berghoff, Esser, Garten Brau, and New Glarus. It also continues to curry favor with the old-timers by stocking Blatz and Old Milwaukee. Check out the changing bumper sticker collection on the beer cooler.

The bike trail crew also required that the Riley Tavern improve on typical tavern standards for nonalcoholic beverages. Biking families are an important part of that crowd, so there is a selection of mineral water, caffeine-free pop, and juice. A light menu of sandwiches and soup specials satisfies appetites. Surprises pop up on the Friday menu.

Fridays and Saturdays sometimes bring crowds taxing Riley Tavern's facilities. This is especially true on music nights. A blues band on a summer night can mean overflow crowds sitting on the grass outside listening to the music. But it is a congenial outdoor concert atmosphere in which leather-clad bikers and suburban moms get along fine.

I'm still partial to the Riley on its lazier and hazier afternoons. The place is quiet, held down by some grizzled locals who love to tease visiting bicyclists, and altogether fit for the contemplation of a tall, cool one. This is an indispensable stop on the local "tour de bars" that includes Pine Bluff, Blue Mounds, and Ridgeway. Many a line of biker (we're talking Hog version) bar lore has been slammed down by bards of the Harley-Davidson school.

▼ ▼ ▼ ▼ ▼ ▼ ▼ ▼ ▼ ▼ ▼ ▼ ▼ ▼ ▼ ▼ ▼ ▼

Watertown

F. W. Webb Pub and Eatery
403 E. Main Street
(920) 262-9560

Webb's became the talk of Milwaukee's transit-inclined beer-drinking crowd in the summer of 1998 because of the state-funded commuter train experiment. What a surprise for transportation planners! Not only did the suit-and-briefcase crowd use the train to travel to Milwaukee's office buildings, but city folks used the train to visit small-towns and sample local culture. This enabled many under-60 folks to experience for the first time the very rewarding European experience of pub visits followed by a comfortable train ride home.

Well, the transit experiment is over (with hope of restoration), but Webb's continues to draw locals and beer drinkers from Milwaukee and Waukesha. Many come to sample from among the almost 80 bottled brews in a very well balanced collection. But don't forget taps: Newcastle, Leinenkugel, Hacker-Pschorr, Paulaner, and a rotating selection of standard domestics.

The spot is a great fit for Watertown's thoroughly German heritage. As one local put it: "It's about time we get good beer back here." The fact that Watertown is so steeped in German history surprises many who know that Milwaukee was a German-American Athens. The past heritage of a lively German-language press, debating societies, and all manner of fraternal groups has been a long-muffled plea for a decent beer. The ghosts of the old August Fuermann brewery must be pleased.

As often happens, beer drinkers sample the menu and find additional reasons to visit. In Webb's case there are good deli sandwiches and a real fish boil. The locals appreciate the tasteful renovation of what was pretty much a run-of-the-mill bar under three or four past names. In a move that it is hoped will be emulated by taverns everywhere, glass blocks made way for a large window. And, to cap it off, Webb's has gone officially nonsmoking—a move that should pull folks in from Madison and elsewhere as soon as the word gets out.

▼ ▼ ▼ ▼ ▼ ▼ ▼ ▼ ▼ ▼ ▼ ▼ ▼ ▼ ▼ ▼ ▼ ▼

Whitewater
Randy's Fun Hunters Brewery
841 E. Milwaukee Street
(262) 473-8000

Randy's occupies a location that has served thirsty and hungry travelers since the end of Prohibition. Additions, remodeling, and changes in ownership during almost every generation have not lessened its following among those taking the Highway 12 tour from northern Illinois to Madison. Although the bar was more or less an adjunct to Randy's restaurant until a 1989 fire, the addition of brew pub facilities put the liquid refreshment end of the business on equal footing with the food and banquet side.

House brews include nine distinct types: amber lager, golden pilsner, red bock, brown ale, Oktoberfest, wheat ale, oatmeal stout, winter lager, and pale ale. Not all are brewed year-round, so check the brews of the day or call ahead. But it must be admitted that UW-Whitewater students and faculty seem content to follow the seasonal flow.

There is a hearty little band of home brewers who make this a home away from home. If you run into them, you'll find some of them picky beyond all belief, but still finding brews among Randy's that get their seal of approval. Maybe it's kind of a game to them. Maybe they were goading me into a defense of Berghoff, New Glarus, and Brewery Creek beers (all of which need no defense). If they mess with you, tell them to start their own damn brew pub.

As for food, customers give Randy's very high marks. The menu is extensive—35 entrees, salads, sandwiches, a baked French onion soup specialty, and many appetizers. Daily specials, weekend prime rib, and Sunday brunch round out the well-received fare. This is one of those places where beer lovers start to worry that the food will take the spotlight away from the beer. Well, we won't let that happen, will we?

Southwest Wisconsin

▼ ▼ ▼ ▼ ▼ ▼ ▼ ▼ ▼ ▼ ▼ ▼ ▼ ▼ ▼ ▼ ▼ ▼ ▼

When southwest Wisconsin is mentioned, geologists and outdoorspeople immediately think of the state's unglaciated driftless region and the coulees of the Mississippi River valley. According to the information put out for visitors by the Department of Tourism, this region of the state is a mix of driftless topography with some of Wisconsin's central sands and a bit of prairie country thrown in.

In many ways it is the area least familiar to travelers. Yet its boundaries include such well-known destinations as the House on the Rock and the Lake Delton attractions just west of Wisconsin Dells. It is a historic and long-settled area of Wisconsin, although it remains predominantly rural and can claim only La Crosse as a larger city.

Some tavern-savvy observers believe that it is the area least friendly to taverns, the recent past offering the anomaly of "dry" towns in Wisconsin and overzealous regulators of all stripes. But it is a rule happily eroded by the exceptions of lively tavern culture in places like Blanchardville, Highland, Hollandale, Muscoda, New Glarus, and Ridgeway, and the impressive party reputation of La Crosse.

The mixed reputation may have something to do with history and settlement patterns. It is the Wisconsin area least German and Nordic, with many of its earliest pioneers originating in the upper South. Yet its unusual ethnic stew of Scots, Welsh, and Cornish were known to hoist a brew or two after a day in the region's lead mines. So much so that the rough-and-tumble of those mining towns attracted many a reforming preacher. Strong antitavern sentiment in some churches continues to color local politics in parts of the region.

These historical factors notwithstanding, there are still plenty of taverns worthy of note, a great deal of beer-drinking tradition, and some positive trends. A lightly populated area that has lost many of its farms and cheese factories, it is fortunate to retain many of its classic rural taverns. It boasts a history of Wisconsin's first brewery (Mineral Point), the ruins of a once renowned regional brewery (Potosi), and the home of the state's longest-surviving brewery (Joseph Huber in Monroe).

In many parts of the area, the unfriendliness of conservative rural town government resulted in a clustering of taverns in the villages and small cities. This in turn added taverns to the list of "going into town" spots for rural dwellers and created routines of after-milking breakfast specials that persist in many taverns. The clustering has also created an informal pattern of pub crawling that is common on Friday, Saturday, and holiday nights. Called "cruising," "making the rounds," "doing the strip," and other names, the custom leads patrons to circulate between taverns that are within walking distance.

The clusters of village taverns also take on added life during the many festivals that southwest Wisconsin hosts. Check your visitor guides for calendars of events relating to mushroom gathering, apple harvest, antique farm equipment field days, and frontier reenactments. If you don't mind crowds, those are good days to check out taverns. The La Crosse Oktoberfest is in a class by itself and

▼ ▼ ▼ ▼ ▼ ▼ ▼ ▼ ▼ ▼ ▼ ▼ ▼ ▼ ▼ ▼ ▼ ▼

unrivaled in Wisconsin as a time when the spirit of the community event infuses both the festival grounds and the city's many taverns.

The river town taverns often augment the standard Wisconsin Friday night fish fry with catfish and snapping turtle. Some bars in the Mineral Point area offer the Cornish pasty. Taverns in the area are beginning to expand their offerings of beer and food to cater to visitors. Those in search of deer, turkey, trout, and antiques all have favorite spots. Canoeists, boaters, trail bicyclists, and campers are also a growing part of the customer base in prime recreation zones.

Southwest Wisconsin offers a number of motor routes for tavern touring. Highway 35 from Prairie du Chien to Fountain City is not only a scenic section of the Great River Road, it is also a belt of visitor-friendly taverns. Shorter routes, such as Sauk City–Spring Green–Muscoda and Mineral Point–Hollandale–New Glarus–Monroe, can also position you well for scenic touring and visits to friendly watering holes.

A note of caution: Southwest Wisconsin has more miles of curvy road and unguarded hillside dropoffs than the rest of the state combined. Deer, livestock, farm equipment, and bikers also make driving tricky. Be careful out there.

▼ ▼ ▼ ▼ ▼ ▼ ▼ ▼ ▼ ▼ ▼ ▼ ▼ ▼ ▼ ▼ ▼ ▼

Black River Falls .

Molly's Grill
44 Main Street
(715) 284-9284

Three women friends directed me to Molly's, all the while arguing among themselves whether it is a tavern, a cafe, or a coffee shop. Well, my vote is in: Molly's is a winning combination of all these elements. This establishment is an object lesson in reattracting the lighter-drinking and nondrinking crowds that used to visit the neighborhood bar and grill.

Molly's does not compete with the fully stocked microbrew taverns. Instead it adopts a strategy of "feature beers." This means both seasonal rotation and surprises on a routine basis. The Pioneer Brewery is only a few blocks away on Pierce Street, so the Pioneer amber, pale ale, and seasonals are as fresh as can be found. This bar is one of the most congenial daytime spots I have ever encountered.

On all three of my visits a four-woman crew kept things moving smoothly. One can see a pattern here: I was referred by women to a business staffed by women and named after a legendary local woman. Black River Falls's Molly Brown started as a logging camp cook, married a millionaire and traveled with him until he was killed on an African safari, and returned to her hometown to run a boardinghouse with great food, hospitality, and incredible storytelling. The current namesake does a respectable job of keeping all those traditions well burnished.

Interstate 94 travelers can skip the truck stop on the next trip. Instead, the short detour into Black River Falls will put them in a well-lit spot with a nineteenth-century feel while they eat their burger. Make that burgers. Molly's offers eight different burgers, not to mention 11 appetizers, 12 sandwiches, stir-fry, steaks, Italian entrees, fish fry, daily soups, slice-of-the-day pie (from a list of 25 kinds!), and sundaes and malts. What more could you want? Well, how about omelettes and breakfast specials?

I'm hooked. One visit and you won't zoom past Black River Falls again.

▼ ▼ ▼ ▼ ▼ ▼ ▼ ▼ ▼ ▼ ▼ ▼ ▼ ▼ ▼ ▼ ▼

Boscobel Hotel
1005 Wisconsin Avenue
(608) 375-4714

While travelers may have known this historic site in its former lives, they may not be aware that new owners Jeff and Beth Novinska have undertaken an impressive remodeling job. Some may lament the passing of the blues jams and the solo acoustic guitar acts, but the regulars still keep the spot as congenial a one as you'll find between Muscoda and Prairie du Chien.

As for history, the substantial stone building is a fine example of the first wave of hotels that replaced the ramshackle inns and boardinghouses of early statehood days. The building also has a place in legend and lore. On the prim and proper side, it boasts its status as the birthplace of the Gideon Bible. On the more titillating side, the locals insist that John and Jackie Kennedy conceived a child in an upstairs room during a campaign swing.

The Boscobel Hotel's bar sticks to bottled beer, with roughly 20 types available at any given time. Southern Wisconsin's regionals and micros are usually in the mix. The Novinskas have also reintroduced food for the first time since the hotel's heyday as a lodging place. At my last 1999 visit the menu was still in the experimental and expanding stage but did include locally praised sandwiches and steaks.

Nearly everyone in the lower Wisconsin River valley has a Boscobel Hotel story. Back-to-the-landers from rural Blue River like to recall times in the mid-1980s when two Sandinistas from Nicaragua would visit with a group of weekly newspaper writers, American Indians, and antiforeclosure farm activists. Long-time residents cherish heirloom stories of soldiers seeing off or welcoming back five generations of soldiers. The place is so steeped in history that during the annual Boscobel festival, Civil War reenactors seem like part of the furnishings.

▼ ▼ ▼ ▼ ▼ ▼ ▼ ▼ ▼ ▼ ▼ ▼ ▼ ▼ ▼ ▼ ▼ ▼

Dodgeville

Pat and Mike's
110 Diagonal Street
(608) 935-9380

Want to talk about soccer, savor a juicy burger, and sip a pint of Wisconsin microbrew? Well, if you are in Dodgeville, you are in luck. Pat Halpin, an Irish-American pipefitter, and Mike Surtees, a former investment broker, are the men behind the name. This father-in-law and son-in-law duo account for the deftly combined elements of Chicago neighborhood tavern, sports bar, and British Isles pub.

Their 1995 purchase of the former Buck and Ev's resulted in an extensive makeover. The result: a well-lit and roomy establishment with a 12-sandwich menu and perhaps the most extensive beer list between Madison and Dubuque. Favorites on the menu include the beef patty melt, the grilled Reuben, and the Italian poor boy. Daily specials and a Friday fish fry bring in construction workers and tourists. Also on the menu is a spicy jalapeño popper that is the perfect complement to Leinie's Red.

Beer drinkers appreciate the freshness of the draft beer at Pat and Mike's. Many rural and small-town taverns cannot move enough draft beer to ensure frequent turnover of barrels. No problem at Pat and Mike's; the latest New Glarus offering is always at its best. Recent tap additions include a nitrogen setup for Guinness and Hinterland Pub Draught. The coolers are stacked with a nice variety of bottled beer, including regionals. Many imports are also available. The Newcastle Brown from England is a rare find.

Pat and Mike's has developed a following among Land's End employees. From May through October, an assortment of campers, sportsmen, and day-trip travelers drop by. The bicycles mounted on the vehicles parked outside point out that the western terminus of the Military Ridge Trail is only a mile north on Highway 23. Newcomers can join in the sports talk and the card games. Families are welcome, and women can drink their beers in peace.

Tavern purists have come to consider this spot an oasis in southwest Wisconsin. Many a sales rep has told me this is the place to stop on the Madison-to-Dubuque route. More than a few construction workers down from La Crosse or up from Rockford manage to take advantage of Pat and Mike's hospitality.

▼ ▼ ▼ ▼ ▼ ▼ ▼ ▼ ▼ ▼ ▼ ▼ ▼ ▼ ▼ ▼ ▼

Ferryville
Sportsman's Bar and Grill
Highway 35
(608) 734-3563

There must be hundreds of Wisconsin taverns bearing this name (I've been in several dozen). Many are exclusively male domains. This one will do quite nicely for a family visit, thank you. They keep things simple here with one tap beer (Pabst Blue Ribbon) and a handful of standard brands. And they sell almost as much pop as beer.

It has a fantastic view of the Mississippi River. Autumn leaves and migratory bird pilgrimages provide pleasant clashes of colors and motion. Rail buffs will enjoy the frequent Burlington Northern–Santa Fe action on the main line between the bar and the river. In season, hunters, fishermen, campers, and bird-watchers all pass through on what is called the longest one-street town in America.

Sportsman's is one of the better information spots on this stretch of the great river. Outside of Northwoods lake lodges, this is home to some of the most savvy fishermen in Wisconsin. But if there are six or more locals at the bar you can find out about more than fishing hot spots. Overheard on my last visit: who has apple butter to sell, where to find smoked fish, how to find quilters and potters hidden in the hills, where turkeys are foraging on the bluffs, and which civic group is sponsoring a turtle dinner.

This establishment ranks high on my tall tale index, and I don't just mean fishing stories. Tavern tales thrown my way in this space have included ghosts, legendary trappers, madams of yesteryear, and UFOs. But it absolutely stands out in a category of its own for a chilling tale of a family of local witches.

A café-style menu starts pulling in customers at 6 A.M. The hearty breakfasts are geared to the hunting and fishing crowd. The boating crowd stops in for drinks and sandwiches at lunch. Tourists on the Great River Road (Highway 35) round out the day at dinnertime. The food is standard fare but prepared and served in surroundings cleaner than most "sportsmen's" bars. The catfish dinner has a reputation that reaches from Prairie du Chien to La Crosse.

Fountain City

Monarch Tavern and Preservation Hall

19 N. Main Street

(608) 687-4231

The origins of the Monarch as an Odd Fellows all-male club accounts for the "No Waitresses Since 1894—Order at the Bar" sign. But rest assured, hospitality and gender inclusiveness have improved since then. The 10 P.M. unannounced arrival of our tavern touring group (on its second wind after a visit to La Crosse's Oktoberfest) was met not with a groan but with the re-opening of the kitchen.

We ate at refinished saloon poker tables, quaffed the beers available at that time, and listened to the folk music wafting out of the Preservation Hall dining area. We sampled the contract-brewed Fountain Brew and Prairie Moon Red and pronounced them top-shelf. Since that visit Old Heidelberg, Eagle Valley Harvest Gold, and Fountain Bock have come online. The glowing reports continue.

The place is also gaining fame as an all-around community center, entertainment spot, and visitors' information bureau. The arts run to some alternative fare, with folk music and jazz making a rare small-town appearance. A mention of the spot sent a bike-touring friend on her own expedition. She was pleased to add her endorsement along with a report of memorable conversations with local artists, potters, photographers, and musicians.

The Monarch fits perfectly in this picturesque Mississippi River town. The owners proudly distribute the local boosters walking tour flyer. In good weather, they also cheerfully usher patrons to the beer garden with the river valley view, in spite of the long walk for servers. In a place that has everything to commend it, special note must be made of Bert the cook. It just doesn't get much better than Prairie Moon Red and Bert's Famous Ribs. So come on, Wisconsinites, discover what the good folks from Rochester, Minnesota, have already been sampling on our soil.

▼ ▼ ▼ ▼ ▼ ▼ ▼ ▼ ▼ ▼ ▼ ▼ ▼ ▼ ▼ ▼ ▼

La Crosse

Bodega Brew Pub
122 South Fourth Street
(608) 782-0677

B odega possesses the distinct advantage of a location in the heart of one of the best tavern districts in Wisconsin. The daytime business and student crowd gives way to evening beer drinkers and seekers of jazz and progressive contemporary music. Two full-windowed walls make it the best spot for people watching in Wisconsin's favorite party town. It is ranked above Madison's State Street as the place for postcollegiate types to perform spectator sipping.

During our last visit, the modest in-house brewing gizmo was out of commission. Previous visits had rewarded us with Urban Amber Ale, a pleasing brew with just a bit of edge. Rumor has it that a new seven-barrel brew system will soon be installed.

In the meantime, there are still many treats to sample. The 11 taps with rotated selections do well by the brews pouring forth from New Glarus and Berghoff, with due deference to local Old Style products. The bottled line is creeping up on 200 entries. Those offerings span the distance from Abbaye des Rois to Zywiec Pilsner. Even veteran brown-bottle fans will run into new finds here among both imports and micros. Beer confidence runs so high at Bodega that they have no menu. A few of the bartenders have looked the other way at my smuggled sandwiches or burritos (my cover story is that I'm on a tight business trip schedule and have time for a tavern visit or diner stop, not both).

A nice side benefit to the location is the neighboring business. Red Oak Books and its connected coffee shop attract a nice slice of La Crosse's arts community. A beef farmer touring buddy told me that a poetry reading in a bookstore is a surprise treat after a good strong Scottish ale. The Red Oak/Bodega mix is a nice alternative to the bookstore/bistro/bicycle shop hybrids that tax management expertise. Any combination of beer and books scores points in my book. And since this is my book, consider the points scored.

▼ ▼ ▼ ▼ ▼ ▼ ▼ ▼ ▼ ▼ ▼ ▼ ▼ ▼ ▼ ▼ ▼ ▼

La Crosse

Night Hawks Tap Room
401 S. Third Street
(608) 785-7427

Seven taps with rotating selections pull in the beer drinkers. Wheat beers were hot on my last summer stop at this popular nightspot. And, oddly enough, here in Heileman town, bottled and draft Point beers have a following among the regulars. It has a growing selection of regional brews.

Night Hawks is the type of place that picks up more energy the later it gets. The crowd often grows after midnight. The live music mix includes blues, rock, funk, and more blues. A Wednesday blues jam provides local and national surprises. The band posters bedeck the walls like campaign ribbons.

Those who favor elbow-bending over toe-tapping needn't worry about being blasted out the door on band nights. Night Hawks has one of the best midsize club setups in terms of coexistence of the bar crowd and the music crowd. The bar area is separated from the rear room by a low arched passageway that acts as an acoustic block. If you venture through that portal on a busy night you'll want your dancing shoes.

There is a bit of an age and cultural divide between the front bar and the back dance floor. The bar patrons look to be in their 30s and 40s. The dancers are a bit younger. At the bar a jukebox collection of blues, salsa, jazz, zydeco, and fusion suggests a mellow broad-mindedness.

A bit of candor compels the admission that more than one observer among my mostly male corps of tavern sleuths has remarked that the bartenders here include, year in and year out, some of the most attractive young women in La Crosse. This demonstrates that some tavern owners will make extra efforts to differentiate themselves from the competition. It works here because the bartenders, both men and women, generally know what they're doing.

How about that lava lamp collection behind the bar?

▼ ▼ ▼ ▼ ▼ ▼ ▼ ▼ ▼ ▼ ▼ ▼ ▼ ▼ ▼ ▼ ▼ ▼

La Crosse

Ski's Sports Bar
1031 S. Fourth Street (Fourth and Mississippi)
(608) 782-9055

No Wisconsin tavern guide would be complete without mention of a no-nonsense blue-collar bar across the street from a major industrial facility. At one time you could throw a rock in any Wisconsin city and hit such a place. That was, of course, in a time when neighborhoods and their taverns were built near factories. With city cores abandoned and new industrial parks in cornfields, the old pattern is broken.

Ski's still fits the mold with its placement directly across the street from the G. Heileman Brewery. The south exterior wall sports a large sign for Teamsters Local 1081. Younger folks might want to visit so they can see how taverns looked in the days before potted plants and retro art deco. Not to mention the rare sighting of intact Formica, vinyl, and Naugahyde.

The beer runs heavy toward Old Style and Special Export, with brandy on the side. It's not a sports bar in the current sense of the word. It's a 1960s sports bar, with softball and bowling teams dropping in to catch scores on the tube. Hit the place on the right night and you'll find patrons singing to the oldies on the jukebox.

The very mention of Old Style in the context of taverns across from industrial facilities brings other tavern-impacting trends to mind. As this guide goes to production, the fate of the brewery is unclear. Corporate "rightsizing" and other euphemisms for white-collar looting of our communities has no doubt found its way into the vernacular of Ski's bar patter. No doubt colored by red-hot commentary and anatomically difficult suggestions.

Ski's could end up serving as a miner's canary for the blue-collar tavern in this fair river city. La Crosse has always had a reputation for laid-back labor-management relations, tempered by the bosses' understanding of the Creator-endowed worker's right to leave a bit early on that fishing trip (especially since they were prone to do the same). Let us hope and pray that places like Ski's can retain their mellowness and fun even in the global economy.

▼ ▼ ▼ ▼ ▼ ▼ ▼ ▼ ▼ ▼ ▼ ▼ ▼ ▼ ▼ ▼ ▼ ▼ ▼ ▼

ANOTHER ROUND

Boyer's Favorite Wisconsin Beers

1. Sprecher Amber
2. New Glarus Snowshoe Ale
3. Berghoff Lager
4. Sprecher Winter Brew
5. Green Bay Pub Draught Cream Ale
6. Leinenkugel Red
7. Point Maple Wheat
8. Berghoff Winterfest Hazelnut
9. Garten Brau Dark
10. Gray's Oatmeal Stout

Brewery Creek Inn and Pub

23 Commerce Street
(608) 987-3298
www.brewerycreek.com

B eer drinking in Wisconsin does not get any more history steeped than at Brewery Creek. Just a mug's throw from the site of the first commercial brewery in Wisconsin (circa 1830s). Up the street from the oldest railroad depot in the state. Next door to the unique Foundry Bookstore, an emporium of rare volumes, manuscripts, and maps of the age of exploration in the old Northwest Territory. Across the creek from the old haunted Walker House, site of a territorial-era hanging. Throw in a quaint town of antiques and artisan shops and historic Pendarvis and you'll have as fine a day trip as exists in these parts.

Brewery Creek's "inn" part of the business is a sumptuous bed and breakfast. Open only since July 1997, the seven rooms with fireplaces, whirlpool baths, and computer modems are already heavily booked. Locally supplied farm produce and a wood-fired bake oven make for interesting provisions. Visitors have raved about the portobello mushroom sandwich, the cashew chicken sandwich, and the daily soup specials.

Then there's beer. Mahogany ale, an amber, and a pleasing *kolsch* make up the initial brews. Porters and stouts are on the drawing board. The expectation is production at levels sufficient to supply selected local taverns. It has been supplementing the house brews with some New Glarus products.

While you're in Mineral Point, make the High Street pub crawl. It's an interesting mix of shot-and-a-beer joints and restored nineteenth-century buildings. I'm partial to Riki's, Tailgaters, and the Royal Inn.

The effort to run a quiet B&B makes for some limited hours in the brew pub. It is not unusual to find it closed at 10 P.M. even on Saturday night. Make this stop part of a day trip plan or call ahead for evening hours.

▼ ▼ ▼ ▼ ▼ ▼ ▼ ▼ ▼ ▼ ▼ ▼ ▼ ▼ ▼ ▼ ▼ ▼

Mondovi

The White Pig
134 W. Main Street
(715) 926-4442

Hunters in Buffalo County make this bar the perennial home of impressive buck contests. But when an informant told me this is *the* deer hunters' bar, I was somewhat skeptical. One visit convinced me, however, that the patrons' blood does indeed run blaze orange. There are few other places where the gray beards make the hunting stories so entertaining. It is a place that grandfathers take grandsons to initiate them. Yes, it's a "guy thing."

The best time to visit is just after deer season (you won't find these fellows warming bar stools while there are permits to be filled). That's the best time to hear a fresh batch of stories. On my visit, I watched a young man hold a group spellbound as he described in whispered tones a two-hour-long stalking of a big buck in standing corn. Listeners heard the wind rustle dried tassels, felt the hunter's quickened pulse, and flinched at the bowstring's release. The storyteller shook his head and grinned, "Boy, that'll make a fellow thirsty." A listener bought him a beer.

It would appear that the main beverages here are draft Leinenkugel's and Sprecher root beer, although other standard brands are available in bottles. Nonhunters visit to take in the unusual collection of pigs. That's right, pigs. Ceramic pigs, plastic pigs, wooden pigs, inflatable pigs, fuzzy stuffed pigs, and a neon pig light.

▼ ▼ ▼ ▼ ▼ ▼ ▼ ▼ ▼ ▼ ▼ ▼ ▼ ▼ ▼ ▼ ▼

Monroe
Baumgartner's Cheese Store and Tavern
1023 16th Avenue
(608) 325-6157

It doesn't get any more Wisconsin than cheese and beer. Throw in a little leberwurst and, some would say, you have the quintessential tavern of the Badger State. Oddly enough, many in nearby Illinois would agree. Thus the anomaly that one of Wisconsin's best-known and most beloved taverns is not familiar to Wisconsin tavern fans outside the southcentral part of the state.

Baumgartner's is, in a way, the home base for the Huber/Berghoff lines. It probably taps out more Huber and Huber Bock than any other bar in the world. Berghoff is well represented with three to five taps depending on the season, including brews that are not seen on tap elsewhere. Bottled New Glarus and Gray's brews are also on hand.

The sociology of Baumgartner's is as impressive as the tavern's credentials. On weekdays there is a sizable lunch crowd. The nights belong to serious beer drinkers. I have seen nine pitchers of beer on the bar for ten patrons on a Friday night. But never fear, the crowd is well mannered. On Saturday, the tourists—from motorhome tourers to Golden Wing motorcyclists—take over. One still hears an occasional comment dropped in *schweitzer deitsch* (Swiss German dialect), though not like years ago. "*Buebe*" demarks the men's room just as it does in many *schtubbe* in the Alps. Swiss maps, heralds, and murals decorate the walls.

And the cheese! The front of the building handles the retail and mail order trade. The tavern specialty is the sturdy cheese sandwich: brick, cheddar, Swiss, and the not-for-the-timid limburger. Combination sandwiches feature hard salami or braunschweiger. Even the deli-style sandwiches come with a slice of brick on the side. The store portion also offers Gruyère, baby Swiss, Gouda, Edam, Havarti, and an award-winning pesto cheese, with basil and pine nuts.

The real test of intestinal fortitude comes in the form of the ultimate Monroe sandwich: limburger, braunschweiger, raw onion, and horseradish mustard on rye. Darn tasty with a pint of Berghoff Maibock. And, oddly enough, the subject of some ribald remarks that do not bear repeating in a guidebook.

For a real slice of ethnic Americana with your cheese, stop in at midafternoon on a weekday and eavesdrop on the cardplaying old-timers. They are steeped in the folkways and seasonal rhythms of their Swiss forebears.

▼ ▼ ▼ ▼ ▼ ▼ ▼ ▼ ▼ ▼ ▼ ▼ ▼ ▼ ▼ ▼ ▼ ▼

Muscoda

Nordic Inn
Junction of Highways 60 and 80 (on the north bank of the Wisconsin River)
(608) 739-3150

Want to rub elbows and bend elbows with loggers? Southwest Wisconsin's hardwood loggers have a reputation for knowing the best taverns in the area. A logging rig in a bar's parking lot, like a semi in front of a café, is supposed to be a good omen. Tavern patrons in the Muscoda area find even more comfort in the fact that the Kever logging family took over the Nordic Inn. Sam and Lynette Kever have brought stability and new features to the Nordic Inn after a number of ownership changes.

A onetime favorite among outdoor enthusiasts, the Nordic Inn's offerings of food, lodging, and drink failed to fire on all cylinders in the mid-1990s. After the Kevers' takeover in 1997, hunters, fishermen, canoeists, and snowmobilers found the earlier full range of service restored and improved upon. Motel bars are seldom worthy of note and rarely rate praise beyond sparing weary travelers the hassles of going out in the evening. But the Kevers have created a genuine tavern environment that draws local patrons from a four-county area.

The beer selection varies and is based primarily on the national brands. However, there are usually a number of Wisconsin regional beers and at least one good draft beer available. Draft root beer is also sold by the mug. The restaurant started out serving only the breakfast and lunch trade, but popular demand soon had it offering the traditional Friday and Saturday night one-two punch of fish and prime rib. The locals love it. Show up at the right time in May and you may see morel mushrooms on the menu.

The location is great—only a hundred yards from the north bank of the Wisconsin River (across from the Village of Muscoda). It is the closest tavern to the river west of Sauk City. It sits at the junction of two of southern Wisconsin's great touring roads: Highway 60 from Prairie du Sac to Prairie du Chien and Highway 80 from Hillsboro to Hazel Green.

▼ ▼ ▼ ▼ ▼ ▼ ▼ ▼ ▼ ▼ ▼ ▼ ▼ ▼ ▼ ▼ ▼

Necedah

Star Route Lounge
Highway 21 West
(608) 565-2461

Patrons of the Star Route Lounge know the marsh country. The place draws a robust crowd formed by the tough economic realities of the central sands region. Outdoorspeople of all stripes stop in, but the bow hunter contingent seems particularly strong. Thus, Star Route is not the place for you if you are offended by the sight of bloodied hunting knives strapped to camouflage-clad legs. In season, there are few places where the hunting stories run as thick and as colorful.

Locals head here for steaks and Leinie's Red. The second meal of choice after a day in the woods is the "Gator Kabob," a combination of vegetables, beef, pork, and alligator. Regulars also praise the fresh-cut french fries.

It appears that there is generally a differentiation in the crowd at Star Route: nondrinkers do not sit at the bar and nurse sodas or coffee. These milder pursuits are relegated to the dining area. The beer and brandy drinkers hold sway at the bar and are often exuberant. Those with delicate ears should be forewarned about occasional rough language, but it doesn't appear personalized or threatening.

There is no desire to be trendy here. Strangers still buy each other drinks here. The bartender will sell you a camouflage shirt if you need one. And if you are in the mood, you can drop quarters in the jukebox and play some polkas.

The culture is more central sands than driftless, with the feel of swamps, tamaracks, and jack pines oozing out of the hardscrabble bachelors who make their weekly tavern pilgrimage here and to other scattered backcountry bars in Juneau County. They love to regale visitors with stories about city folk swallowed up by the marshes. They even steered me to a cute story about a half man, half pig creature said to inhabit the abandoned farms near Sprague.

▼ ▼ ▼ ▼ ▼ ▼ ▼ ▼ ▼ ▼ ▼ ▼ ▼ ▼ ▼ ▼ ▼ ▼

New Diggings

New Diggings General Store and Inn
County Highway W (south side of road)
(608) 965-3231

Southwest Wisconsin has a venerable tradition of store tavern spots that combined both functions from the outset or that evolved from stores into taverns. Here in a forgotten corner of Wisconsin, there is a clear feeling that such establishments are the descendants of the early territorial trading posts. The New Diggings General Store and Inn is only a few miles from where Jesse Shull set up the Old Ouiskonsin Fort and Trading Post for the Hudson Bay Company in the early 1820s.

The antique and collectible furnishings lend to the feeling of historical continuity. The large cast-iron woodstove in the middle of the main bar space warms patrons in the cold parts of the year, while the warm season finds them outside in a beer garden surrounded by the abandoned ghost town buildings of New Diggings.

This beer-only tavern is almost better known by Dubuque, Iowa, and Galena, Illinois, residents than by Wisconsinites. They come for the music and easy sociability. Bands play every Saturday night (9 P.M. to 1 A.M.) and Sunday afternoon (3:30 P.M. to 7:30 P.M.). No tap beer, but a bottled lineup that includes the standard big brands plus Leinie's, Berghoff, New Glarus, Sam Adams, Harp, and jugs of Mississippi Mud Black and Tan.

They're very history-minded at the General Store and Inn, offering books for sale on local traditions and dispensing legend and lore. Their motto is "where the moon is always full," suggesting both the celebratory mood of the establishment and the mythic quality of a town that in the 1830s had a bigger population than Chicago in those days. Now, New Diggings is down to a few houses, a group of dilapidated buildings, and two taverns. That's right, across from the General Store and Inn is another "General Store" that serves a somewhat younger crowd and confuses first-time visitors. That's OK—it's worth a visit, too.

▼ ▼ ▼ ▼ ▼ ▼ ▼ ▼ ▼ ▼ ▼ ▼ ▼ ▼ ▼ ▼ ▼

Glarner Stube
518 First Street
(608) 527-2216

If your budget comes up a little too lean to visit alpine taverns around Zurich and Lucerne, don't worry, a trip to the Glarner Stube in New Glarus will put you in a yodeling mood. Many Green County taverns have a Swiss flavor to them. But in New Glarus, the taverns run like the proverbial Swiss watch. Few small towns boast as many quality taverns. In addition to the Glarner Stube, visitors will find that Puempel's Tavern, the New Glarus Hotel, Sportsmen's Bar and Grill, Burreson's, and the Four Corners Tavern are all worth a visit.

So what distinguishes the Glarner Stube? For starters, the bar is a warm little wood-paneled space with piped-in Swiss accordion music to put you immediately in the throes of central European gemütlichkeit (genial hospitality). A low arched entrance leads to the dining area, *die Stube* (in German, literally, the room), which is filled with intriguing kitchen smells. In New Glarus, taverns are *CLEAN*, service is *EFFICIENT*, and the bartenders and waitstaff are *COURTEOUS*. The Glarner Stube takes these standard Swiss attributes and adds its own expertise. They know the little touches: beer is tapped properly and without excessive head, the bar is wiped after each refill, the ventilation system whisks away tobacco odors, and the wait staff keeps you posted on seating and order progress with the precision of German train conductors.

In the Glarner Stube, the main beer offerings are from the New Glarus Brewing Company less than a mile away. Six to eight bottled European imports are also usually available. Standard American beers are also available but are tastefully hidden out of sight (also no neon, garish logos, or hovering oversize plastic mascots). The bar also sports a decent selection of cordials and liquors. The bartenders have a good reputation as cocktail mixers.

An unusual feature (but consistent with the Swiss passion for caffeine) is found in the Glarner Stube's coffee drinks. Amaretto, brandy, Chambord, Frangelico, Kahlua, kirsch, peppermint schnapps, and whiskey all come into play. Many customers favor the nonalcoholic cappuccino and espresso.

Glarner Stube offers a sturdy lunch and dinner menu. The fondue special is a patron favorite. The Swiss fried potatoes are a delight. Go during the off-season if you hope to savor a leisurely beer and a *wurstsalat*. Or jostle with the summer and fall tourists. You just might meet some Swiss, German, or Austrian visitors.

▼ ▼ ▼ ▼ ▼ ▼ ▼ ▼ ▼ ▼ ▼ ▼ ▼ ▼ ▼ ▼ ▼

Platteville

Hoist House
90 N. Second Street
(608) 348-7819

Downtown Platteville has as hefty a district of college bars as any of the smaller cities hosting University of Wisconsin system campuses. UW-Platteville students are a major influence in many of these spots, but not so much that older nonacademic types are unwelcome. That's especially true of the Hoist House, which draws beer drinkers from surrounding towns like Lancaster, Fennimore, and Mineral Point.

Over the last several years, it has steadily added taps until they're now at 11. The usual lineup includes Gray's, multiple Leinie's, Berghoff, Sam Adams, Woodchuck Draft Cider, and macrobrews. The coolers hold approximately 30 imports.

The "hoist" in the establishment's name is a reference to the crude elevators in the area's old lead and zinc mines. The vintage tile floor and stamped-metal ceiling lends credence to the many stories of the Hoist House serving as a rough-and-tumble pre-Prohibition bar that could be exited via a tunnel. A few of the regulars mentioned that previous generations of UW-Platteville alumni would remember the tavern as a party bar called the Black Cat.

The routine for a Platteville pub crawl with the Hoist House as a starting point varies depending on your age and academic standing. Hoist House is one of the few spots that draws both a wide age spectrum and a fair town-and-gown sampling. The over-30 crowd often gravitates to the veterans posts and supper clubs. Those comfortable in the student mix usually stay right in the tavern district clustered in the few blocks around the Hoist House.

Football-related events break this cycle come late summer and fall. The Chicago Bears training camp draws plenty of Illinois residents and blows the bar scene wide open. It's a good time to start a football argument in Platteville. Home games for UW-Platteville also spread a festive mood townwide.

▼ ▼

ANOTHER ROUND
Beer Events in Wisconsin

Be sure to call ahead for the exact dates.

January

Ice Cold Brewers Fest
Minocqua (715) 358-3040

February

Beer Lovers Brewfest
Manitowoc (920) 683-3926

March

Blessing of the Bock
Milwaukee (414) 645-1580

April

Gitchee Gumee Beer Fest
Superior (715) 394-7716

May

Point's Spring Festival of Beers
Stevens Point (715) 344-9310

Northeast Wisconsin Beer Festival
Appleton (920) 731-3322

Wisconsin Microbrewers Fest
Chilton (920) 849-2534

June

Summerfest (last week of June and first week of July)
Milwaukee (414) 273-FEST

Southport Micro Beer Festival
Kenosha (262) 694-9050

Essen Haus Bierfest
Madison (608) 258-8619

July

Jaycees Brews and Blues Festival
Oshkosh (920) 235-0605

71

▼ ▼ ▼ ▼ ▼ ▼ ▼ ▼ ▼ ▼ ▼ ▼ ▼ ▼ ▼ ▼ ▼ ▼ ▼

Wisconsin State Fair
West Allis (800) 884-FAIR

Germanfest
Milwaukee (414) 464-9444

August

Great Taste of the Midwest
Madison (608) 249-7126

West Bend Germanfest
West Bend (262) 338-2666

September

Sprecherfest
Milwaukee (414) 297-8000

Taste of Madison
Madison (608) 831-1725

Green Bay Oktoberfest (late September)
Green Bay (920) 437-BEER

Boulder Beer Fest
Boulder Junction (715) 356-9456

Harvest Fair
Milwaukee (414) 266-7000

Appleton Octoberfest
Appleton (920) 734-3377

Gemuetlichkeit Homebrew Competition
Jefferson (920) 674-3843

October

La Crosse Oktoberfest (sometimes starts late September)
La Crosse (608) 784-FEST

Quivey's Grove Beer Fest
Madison (608) 273-4900

Rhinelander Oktoberfest
Rhinelander (800) 236-4386

New Glarus Oktoberfest
New Glarus (800) 527-6838

November

Taste of the World
Green Bay (920) 437-0202

▼ ▼ ▼ ▼ ▼ ▼ ▼ ▼ ▼ ▼ ▼ ▼ ▼ ▼ ▼ ▼ ▼

Prairie du Chien
Winneshiek Bar and Marina
Frenchtown Road
(608) 326-2888

S ummer boating season enlivens many taverns along the Mississippi River. When the bar business goes hand in hand with a marina, the pace is even more frenetic. Boaters, construction workers, salespeople, and campers converge on the Winneshiek in conjunction with their daily rounds.

The bar and marina are of comparatively recent origin, the north fringe of Prairie du Chien being the focus of residential and commercial redevelopment. You might be surprised that the marina is not directly on the big river; Winneshiek is reached via a dredged channel and inlet. The site combines both the good and the bad of locations with growing pains: a nice view of the bluffs in Iowa contrasting with the somewhat neglected restaurant/campground business across the road and an out-of-place mobile home park sitting exposed on the north bank of the marina.

But this is not, after all, a resort. It's a refueling spot. Camping families stop in to get a break from cooking and to let kids watch the boats. Construction workers grab quick lunches. Boaters snatch up takeout food and beverages. Room enough inside and tables enough on an outside deck to serve them all, with space left over for a game to be played on a cribbage board built into the bar surface.

The fare is simple and the beer selection limited (with promises of expansion). The most popular brand of beer here is Ice Cold. Sandwiches for lunch, daily dinner specials, and Friday night fish fries meet boater expectations. The Philly Cheesesteak does not match what this native Pennsylvanian experienced at the hands of Mama Tallarico, but it clearly surpasses other tavern versions.

Note to parents: Winneshiek's is a family-friendly spot. But I did notice, on two separate occasions, that a large ship's figurehead of a bare-chested mermaid seems to startle small children.

▼ ▼ ▼ ▼ ▼ ▼ ▼ ▼ ▼ ▼ ▼ ▼ ▼ ▼ ▼ ▼ ▼ ▼

Reedsburg

Endehouse Brewery and Restaurant

1020 E. Main Street
(608) 524-8600

F ormerly Peterson's Supper Club, in 1996 the Petersons received their brewer's permit and reconfigured the business. It isn't often that a supper club moves toward a more beer-drinker-friendly perspective. But with a motto such as "good for what ales you" and five distinguished brews, it's no longer in the "stuff a prime rib in them and shove them out the door" category. The porter and pale ale are widely respected.

The Endehouse illustrates a brew pub path that makes for smooth transitions and satisfied customers: take an established food business, with a track record for service and good management, and add the brewing capacity. Many brew pubs start from scratch and are attempting to do too many things at the same time. Often, the result is good beer but shoddy service and uneven kitchen results. Not at the Endehouse—it all clicks together.

The oval bar is a good spot for quaffing the brews and relaxing to jazz and big-band tapes. Or, if you've arrived with an appetite, frequent customers recommend the steaks served up in three separate dining areas or outdoor seating in season.

The business next door is an unusual fabric store/quilt shop/craft outlet set in an older residence, with each room devoted to a different part of the color spectrum. Those in the know tell me this store is the place for unique prints to sew drapes, curtains, quilts, and apparel. If you are forced to participate in the "which color looks best" process, you will at least have an opportunity to offset that duty with an Endehouse ale.

▼ ▼ ▼ ▼ ▼ ▼ ▼ ▼ ▼ ▼ ▼ ▼ ▼ ▼ ▼ ▼ ▼

Paradise Lounge
740 Water Street
(608) 643-3422

In a small town blessed with many solid taverns, the Paradise Lounge has the best setting. The bar is on street level, the Riverfront Restaurant is around the back downstairs (a stone's throw from the Wisconsin River), and the Riverview Ballroom is on the same level as the bar and over the restaurant. All three related businesses draw customers on the strength of their respective assets of beer, food, and music. Even the totally independent Jimmy's Bar across the street is kind of an annex on overflow nights (and worthy of a visit on its own merits).

Five taps lead with local New Glarus and Esser's favorites. The bottled selections tally about 20, mostly the standards and some regionals. They also pour a lot of shots here. The conversation is lively and runs through Harleys, pickups, racing, fishing, and hunting. It's a good spot to find out what's happening on this stretch of the Wisconsin River.

But just when you think you've got the place culturally pegged, in will saunter a literary type spouting the praises of August Derleth or an amateur naturalist brimming with the day's joys in the Baraboo hills. During the summer the customer mix is at its absolute quirkiest during the late afternoon and early evening hours. That's when you just might find a grandmother inspecting a brand-new tattoo on a black-clad punker or a construction worker telling a graduate student about a hidden glade with a box turtle population.

You'll find customers from Madison, Portage, and Baraboo when the hot bands drop in. In winter, this is a nice spot to warm up after the traditional eagle-watching days along the river. The Paradise also catches quite a few fall color visitors who run a circuit that starts with the taverns around the Merrimac ferry and continues out to Spring Green. All in all, a nice balance of locals and drop-in visitors.

Sparta

Legion Post 100 Bar
Highway 21 East
(608) 269-4411

I n the Fort McCoy/Camp Douglas area there is no shortage of bars with retired military hardware permanently parked outside. The Army presence and
patriotic heartland values combine to make local veterans clubs a focus for
social life. It is an area where you might sit down to a fish fry in a room full of
camouflage fatigues. The person next to you is as likely to be a National Guard
officer, a reservist pilot, or a crusty career sergeant as a graying veteran of
Omaha Beach.

Sparta's Legion Post 100 Bar is the most representative area tavern catering
to GIs and veterans. Other local taverns may sport names like "The Foxhole" or
decorate with a military theme using combat photographs or ship and aircraft
posters, but Post 100 is open and accessible to nonveterans and nonmilitary
personnel. It is a site of receptions and homespun entertainment. They're also
generous enough to steer you to veterans clubs in Tomah or New Lisbon if a big
dance or benefit dinner will boost comrades in those towns.

Leinenkugel craft brews are the only beers to augment the national brands
and Heileman's lines in Post 100's coolers. But if you stop here it's as much for
the sociology as for the liquid refreshment. It is no secret that the veterans population is an aging one. At one time, many more American Legion and Veterans
of Foreign Wars posts had bars that were open to the public.

Twenty to 30 years ago, many of these veterans posts had bar regulars who
were none too friendly to strangers. Never mind that the only shooting these
bellicose types had witnessed was at the Fort Dix, New Jersey, rifle range. Long
hair, tie-dyed shirts, and alternative political views were not welcome, even if
the bearers of same were still nursing combat wounds. Thankfully, the internal
culture has changed for the better in most of these places (the ones that didn't
change closed for lack of business).

The Sparta post is perhaps unusual in that it hosts quite a few guardsmen,
reservists, and active-duty military in addition to veterans of prior wars, and is
still fairly accepting of the general public. This is not to say that the visitor won't
find some zealous views on foreign policy matters here. And some sensitivity is
called for if a talkative patron evokes a painful memory. A general rule of
thumb in such quarters goes thusly: if you do not know the event under discussion through firsthand experience, don't open your mouth about it.

Check out the military unit ceiling tiles. They also promised me their sur-
plus UH-1 helicopter, or "Huey," would be on display by the time this guidebook is published.

▼ ▼ ▼ ▼ ▼ ▼ ▼ ▼ ▼ ▼ ▼ ▼ ▼ ▼ ▼ ▼

Parlor Bar and Grill
101 East Jefferson Street
(608) 588-2363

S pring Green is one of Wisconsin's classiest small communities and deserves a tavern that measures up to community standards. In the Parlor Bar and Grill it's nice to see people get what they deserve. From the canoe-paddle door handle on the entrance to the spotless glasses and carefully poured taps, you sense a perfect fit for a folksy and artsy town in the lower Wisconsin River valley.

Some say it is here that you will find the freshest Leinenkugel's draft in all of southern Wisconsin. It's no accident, since the Parlor is the proudest booster of the Indian gal label that I encountered in all my tavern tours. Southwest Wisconsin brew partisans needn't worry, New Glarus and Berghoff bottles back up the Leinie's taps.

The Parlor is already a favorite among the tavern-touring crowd. Quite a few beer-savvy folks make this a pit stop on the run between the brew pubs in Reedsburg and Mineral Point. Like Pat and Mike's in nearby Dodgeville, this spot has a following among visitors from Illinois. And like all great taverns, the welcome mat is out for steady customers and first timers.

Few taverns have so many great day trip or camping trip tie-ins. Tower Hill State Park, the Springs Resort, American Players Theater, and the Silver Star Inn B&B are only minutes away. Within walking distance are a number of craft shops and studios. Next door is the Gard Theater, which offers a mix of movies, plays, and live music. I'd be remiss if I didn't mention that Spring Green has a bit of a downtown tavern district, with diverse spots that represent at least four different subcultures. A belt of supper clubs on Highway 14 on the north edge of town provides additional imbibing choices.

Oops, almost forgot, the Parlor Bar and Grill also holds its own on sandwiches and appetizers. The menu is not extensive but is very well received by the tired and grubby canoeists who trudge in at the end of summer days.

▼ ▼ ▼ ▼ ▼ ▼ ▼ ▼ ▼ ▼ ▼ ▼ ▼ ▼ ▼ ▼ ▼ ▼

Trempealeau

Trempealeau Hotel
150 Main Street
(608) 534-6898

Here's another scenic Mississippi River spot that our Gopher neighbors to the west have discovered before the homebred Badgers. And why not? Acts like Arlo Guthrie, Marshall Tucker, Ozark Mountain Daredevils, Floyd Westerman, and Country Joe McDonald will sometimes do an intimate performance here on a Saturday night after playing a big hall in the Twin Cities on Friday.

But if the music is what originally pulls folks in, it's the bar, food, and lodging that keeps them coming back. Leinie's taps keep the locals happy, while bottled Sierra Nevada, Black Dog, Samuel Adams, and Summit selections fill the needs of Minnesotans. About a dozen imports are kept on hand for southern Wisconsinites who happen to stumble in. Tasty appetizers (walnut balls) and desserts (sour cream poppyseed cake and Swedish apple pie) have richly deserved reputations.

This is a place that is classy without being upscale and casually elegant without being prissy. The customer mix is often dictated by music events and the ebb and flow through town. But even jam-packed with brokers, bikers, and bluesmen, it is Wisconsin at its best elbow-rubbing and elbow-bending form.

The Trempealeau Hotel is a perfect end destination or layover spot for a tavern tour. Seven rooms upstairs and a cottage by the river provide comfy lodging. Be advised: this will not be a restful stop for light sleepers or those who go to bed early. Sleeping patterns must be geared to bar hours and freight train schedules. Bring your earplugs.

Northwest Wisconsin

▼ ▼ ▼ ▼ ▼ ▼ ▼ ▼ ▼ ▼ ▼ ▼ ▼ ▼ ▼ ▼ ▼ ▼

This is wild and woolly tavern territory. The area is flush with lodge-style taverns, old roadhouses, tarpaper-shack beer joints, and lakeside bars. The cities and villages are home to many gritty but friendly taverns in the shadows of warehouses and grain elevators.

Much of the area is hardscrabble country. Farms in the old pine forest area struggle, and in many parts of the region jobs are scarce even in good times. Grassroots groups fight environmental battles with multinational corporations and federal and state agencies.

Many of the rural sections of this area have very low tavern densities. Many two- and three-tavern villages have been reduced to one. In no other area of the state did I experience as much attrition of taverns I had hoped to list.

On the other hand, northwest Wisconsin is rich with scenic beauty and worthy destinations. The Upper Mississippi and St. Croix rivers provide continuation of the Highway 35 tour that begins in southwest Wisconsin and has many quaint river town taverns from Bay City to St. Croix Falls. The Chippewa flowage and Lac Courte Oreilles vicinity have an abundance of vintage resort bars. Highway 13 from west of Stratford to Superior, including the Bayfield to Port Wing loop, offers small town after small town of rustic bars.

The bigger population centers have their own tavern assets. Eau Claire has a bustling downtown tavern district and many respectable neighborhood establishments. Chippewa Falls bears the imprint of the local Leinenkugel brewery and still has a number of unrestored taverns that are prized for their authentic pre–World War II feel. Superior is in a class by itself as a modest-sized city, international port of call, and neighbor to Duluth, Minnesota. The campuses of Menominee and River Falls add youthful spice to the taverns of those two communities.

As for the smaller cities and villages, there are some with notable reputations for tavern hospitality. They may not have all the amenities and options of their urban cousins, but they do score well on the fellowship and fun scale. Worthy of mention are Neillsville, Hudson, Ashland, Spooner, Hayward, and Washburn.

The tiny out-of-the-way places are also worthy of the explorer's time and effort. Small taverns run by folksy eccentrics can be found throughout northwest Wisconsin. Many last only a few seasons before restless owners decide to try their hands at other businesses. Such spots do not lend themselves to guidebook parameters. But I'd be remiss if I didn't leave readers something to discover and claim as their own. Enjoy.

▼ ▼ ▼ ▼ ▼ ▼ ▼ ▼ ▼ ▼ ▼ ▼ ▼ ▼ ▼ ▼ ▼ ▼

Bruce

McGinty's Log Bar
Highway 40—Main Street
(715) 868-4635

Don't look for a log building. More than one seeker has been thrown off by this assumption. The exterior blends right into a block of local businesses. The inside is the log lodge. The 1950s vintage log motif runs throughout McGinty's, with a log cabin walk-in cooler, log back bar, and log arches over the restrooms and game room. The contrasts between the standard commercial exterior and Northwoods interior are thrown into further relief by a ceiling covered with carpet square remnants.

It doesn't get much folksier than McGinty's. The bartenders are at ease in modest conversation, and the patrons can regale you with classic Northwoods tales of winter's rigors. One regular likes to poke fun at tipsy snowmobilers and has a repertoire of macabre anecdotes about high-speed encounters with fences and utility poles. One summer seasonal visitor kept our tavern tour entourage in stitches for an hour with his nonstop Ole and Lena jokes in a Norwegian accent.

A visit is instructive about both the sturdiness of the north's small towns and the economic forces and lack of opportunities in rural areas bypassed by tourism. The spot is off the beaten path of today's tourist who is zipping northward to a timeshare or a casino. But there was a time when beat-up boats were towed behind beat-up station wagons, exploring for little-fished lakes and seldom-visited taverns. It's still that sort of place.

The beverage selection is modest: national brands, Milwaukee's Best, Grain Belt, and the Leinie's line. Also, champagne by the bottle! The one-item menu delivers a serviceable homemade hot beef sandwich.

McGinty's is the type of Northwoods tavern that served as the model two generations ago. Now such places are endangered. Visit them while they still exist!

▼ ▼ ▼ ▼ ▼ ▼ ▼ ▼ ▼ ▼ ▼ ▼ ▼ ▼ ▼ ▼ ▼ ▼

Chippewa Falls

Bogies Bar
353 E. Canal Street
(715) 723-9959

Locals laugh when asked how to get to Bogies Bar. One wag suggested that if I drove around awhile I would eventually find it. All I can say is you might want to make your first visit before sundown. You can see the tavern from Chippewa Falls' main bridge, but when you take the off-ramp you must backtrack through residential neighborhoods.

It's worth the search if you like solid blue-collar bars with plenty of conversation. The talk runs through sports, fishing, movies, and music. Regulars will ask "where ya from" and "watcha do." The crowd arrives in groups, but they are not particularly clannish. It is a popular spot among working-class women.

The mood is rock-and-roll jukebox, pool shooting, and shots and beers. Definitely not a fern bar, Bogies Bar stands in contrast to the young-adult takeover of Chippewa Falls' downtown bars. A clean and sparkly bartop surface embedded with seashells and silver coins contrasts nicely with the updated honky-tonk feel. A visit on a Friday night can serve as a reminder of what a neighborhood tavern can do without the frills.

Quite a few of the men that I met here were truckers, mechanics, and construction workers. The women tended to claim assembly work and health care as their job domains. They tend not to talk shop; the job stuff comes up only by way of identifying with "regular folks." These younger workers are very open with their healthy skepticism about their parents' belief in paternalistic corporations and see their own economic security in terms of skills they possess, not loyalty conferred. They acquainted me with an emerging oral tradition that is picking up steam among Generation Xers: the job horror story. The little tales, told in competitive style, bring a laughable one-upmanship to the claims of worst boss, worst day at work, and worst coworker.

Stop in and ventilate about the biggest horse's behind in your work life.

▼ ▼ ▼ ▼ ▼ ▼ ▼ ▼ ▼ ▼ ▼ ▼ ▼ ▼ ▼ ▼ ▼

Chippewa Falls

Mr. C's
32 W. Spring Street
(715) 723-3009

I f you've tired of shiny chrome and brass, upscale hors d'oeuvres, and trendy crowds puffing on $10 cigars, Mr. C's is the antidote for your weltschmerz. This is not to say that the downtown Chippewa Falls bar is a dive (unless you've had your shoes lock up on sticky linoleum in a dimly lit joint and discovered that you've just sat on both a lit cigarette and an unidentifiable gelatinous mass, well, you don't know dives). No, this is simply a timeworn classic with a timeworn crowd (hey, it happens to us all!).

Mr. C's represents the last stand of age against the youth trends that have overcome its neighboring downtown bars. Those who are graying and expanding in the middle are still welcome in these parts. Because of the age demographics, the peak time to visit is from lunch to 6 P.M. The place often clears out by 10 P.M., even on Saturday nights.

It's the type of place that would do nicely as a set for film noir—dim, quiet, and a bit hazy. This is where Chippewa Falls over-the-hill private detectives would go for a shot and a beer if the town still had a fedora-sporting hardboiled P.I. It could still be the sort of place to overhear things you're not supposed to hear. Hard-luck cases who show up in the obituaries are eulogized and toasted after a fashion here.

Old-timers will remember this location as the former Ed's Bar. It's still the same sort of place, except that the current owner also buys and sells antiques at this site. You're forewarned, don't trip over the recent auction acquisitions. Beer-drinking variety here is a matter of which type of Leinie's you want. Delicate ears should note a tradition of female bartenders as salty as night court bailiffs.

▼ ▼ ▼ ▼ ▼ ▼ ▼ ▼ ▼ ▼ ▼ ▼ ▼ ▼ ▼ ▼ ▼

Eau Claire

Mandarin Club's Express Bar

201 E. Lake Street
(715) 836-9111

Bars in Chinese restaurants usually rank at about the same level as motel lobby bars. Finding one that does justice to the bar end of the business, beyond serving as the restaurant's source of Tsing Tao and plum wine, is a near miracle. Discovering that it has a lively crowd of regulars, good music, and a dance floor seems like something out of science fiction. Yet the Express Bar does deliver all these things in a sparkling, renovated environment.

A modest selection of bottled imports, a growing collection of regionals, and all the standard brands of beer make up barley pop offerings here. The Express Bar's mixed drinks are popular among the younger clientele and are served up with flair if you connect with the right bartender. One bartender told me they move a high volume of nonalcoholic drinks as well, not only NA beer, but mineral water and juice for the dance-til-you-drop crowd.

In much of the music department, the crowd leans toward college students. But it does offer some blues, some Grateful Dead knockoffs, and eclectic bands out of the Twin Cities. The music side of the business is in the hands of those familiar with the club scenes in Madison, Milwaukee, and Minneapolis. It's definitely different than the sturdy corner bars of the Chippewa Valley.

It stands out in comparison to most of the college bars—a little less foolishness, none of the goofy frat-boy regurgitation, and more of a serious evening-out feel. Combined with the dining side, it offers a slightly different take on nightclubbing. Two first-time visitors observed that the mood is closer to Milwaukee's Water Street than Eau Claire's beer joints.

The word has definitely gotten out, so it's not unusual to run into young professionals from Black River Falls, Rice Lake, and Hudson who decide to sample Eau Claire's nightlife when they aren't up for the Twin Cities. It's one of the more uncommon offerings in northwest Wisconsin and worth a visit if you're in town for the evening.

▼ ▼ ▼ ▼ ▼ ▼ ▼ ▼ ▼ ▼ ▼ ▼ ▼ ▼ ▼ ▼ ▼

Eau Claire
Northwoods Brew Pub and Grill
3560 Oakwood Mall Drive
(715) 552-0511
www.northwoodsbrewpub.com

E ven true-blue bar stool denizens will be tempted to repair to the stuffed chairs in the large space off to the side of the bar. There, a fireplace and warm log walls transport you to that Northwoods lodge all true Wisconsinites have in their mind's eye. During my visit I spotted several patrons reading newspapers and books—a sure sign that customers feel at home.

It's easy to fall into gender-differentiation traps when talking about taverns in general and brew pubs in particular. Even though many women like the brew pub atmosphere, cultural and personal-safety issues often act to discourage women from visting many brew pub sites. That phenomenon is most obvious when the brew pub sits in a dark warehouse district or in an urban core. The Northwoods Brew Pub and Grill location does appeal to women on several counts. The location in a shopping center area makes for easy access and easy parking. Not to mention that it makes a great lunchtime or after-work stop in the midst of errands to bookstores, gift shops, and pharmacies. Patterns of business location have been altered by automobile culture, and here's one bit of evidence that our beer emporiums may undergo that shift, too.

The Northwoods Brew Pub is noted for several distinctive year-round brews. Half Moon Gold is a light-bodied ale. Red Cedar Red measures up as an assertive red. Birch Wood Ale is a milder transition ale for those unaccustomed to full-flavored brews. Poplar Porter has just the right "charred" character. Dark Walnut Stout is a milder but complex stout that wins over non–stout drinkers. Spring brings the addition of Wascally Wheat, while summer heralds Honey Wheat.

The menu sports a large appetizer list (including the mysterious Northwoods Oysters). I can vouch for an excellent French onion ale soup and a hearty wild rice soup. Customers comment favorably on the sandwiches and the dinner menu. The atmosphere, the food, and the brew make Northwoods Brew Pub and Grill a must-stop for those traveling Interstate 94.

▼ ▼

ANOTHER ROUND

More Boyer Beer Favorites

Best Day in the Country: Riley Tavern (Verona), Hooterville Inn (Blue Mounds), Thousand Island Bar (Barneveld), Hyde Store (Hyde—north of Ridgeway), Pat and Mike's (Dodgeville), and Brewery Creek Inn and Pub (Mineral Point).

Best Party Town: La Crosse. No question.

Best Beer Value: Huber returnables.

Best Large Outdoor Event: Milwaukee Summerfest.

Best Line of Wisconsin Microbrews: Capital/Garten Brau.

Best Day in the City: Pub crawl of Water Street, Old World Third Street, and S. Second Street in Milwaukee.

▼ ▼ ▼ ▼ ▼ ▼ ▼ ▼ ▼ ▼ ▼ ▼ ▼ ▼ ▼ ▼ ▼

Hayward
Moccasin Bar and Northwoods Wildlife Museum
15806 1st Street (at Highways 27 and 63)
(715) 634-4211

Hold onto your hats here! The angle of this joint is as subtle as a two-by-four between the eyes. I'd be the first to admit that many of my referrals in this guidebook are based on nuances that are seldom detected in the casual one-stop. Even if your hearing isn't what it used to be, your bifocals call out the need to go trifocal, and your regard for popular culture begins and ends with Monday Night Football, you'll "get it" at the Moccasin Bar. Here you won't need the folklorist's persistence to bag an authentic tall tale. Such legends are dripping off the walls.

Moccasin Bar approaches its task with tongue firmly in cheek. The bar is a fun spot, and its "museum" display cases are a hoot. The P. T. Barnum tradition is alive and well with oddities, straightforward trophies, and thigh-slappers among the exhibits. On the one hand are items like the largest mounted muskie, albino mammals, owls, and commemorative rifles. On the other hand are bizarre stuffed-animal scenes, with raccoons bedecked in jewelry and foxes in courtrooms. In between you will find real-life accounts of renowned fishing guides and epic man-versus-fish struggles in framed clippings.

The displays guarantee a constant stream of visitors that include vanloads of children, grandmothers in walkers, and gawking city folk. The fishermen and duck hunters sit at the bar while the music blares. Throw in a bank of video games and two pool tables and you end up with a bazaar of sights and sounds. Part of the crowd spills over from the attached *Northern Exposure*–style eatery called the Moose Cafe.

You won't find a busier bar on a Sunday morning, although it's lively the rest of the week, too. Regulars stop in for the standard national draft beer on tap. Those of us passing through favor the Leinie's line in bottles. Hard-core sportsmen feast on bar sandwiches and pizzas, but most patrons eat first at the Moose Cafe. The local ritual involves a "shake" of the dice and a $1 mystery shot.

▼ ▼ ▼ ▼ ▼ ▼ ▼ ▼ ▼ ▼ ▼ ▼ ▼ ▼ ▼ ▼ ▼ ▼ ▼

Hudson

Barker's Bar and Grill
413 2nd Street
(715) 386-4123

Readers must be warned that this entry is my way of sneaking in another bar on the Great Tavern Road, otherwise known as Highway 35 or the Great River Road. Some purists might insist that fresh-ground Guatemalan coffee, homemade *pico de gallo* salsa, and a zillion appetizers on a well-stocked menu moves Barker's out of the tavern category. But I would never pass up a place just because it has a daylong flow of sit-down and take-out food customers. The Neanderthals will just have to find their beef jerky, pickled eggs, and generic canned beer elsewhere.

Yes, it is a bar, has a bar to sit at, and has regulars who visit daily for beer. Yes, plenty of beer: 17 taps and 14 bottled brands. Lots of turnover here and local requests. During my fall 1998 visit, a popular draft was St. Croix Maple Ale, and the bartop sported plenty of Moosehead bottles.

And good beer conversation. The regulars include a number of folks who travel far and wide on the brew pub circuit and like to drop in on the microbreweries when they can. This makes for some darn good leads to other nearby towns. Their knowledge base is also extensive about the neighboring watering holes in Minnesota. Here the true-blue brew fans come out before dark, so, unlike in many of my favorite spots, you can sample St. Croix hospitality before the day slips away.

Those expecting a "Northwoods" tavern might be disappointed, though I'd wager they'll get over it real quick. The open "kitchen" behind the bar gives Barker's a snazzy modern diner feel that pulls in Minnesotans and others with tavern phobias. Smoking is not prohibited but is definitely discouraged. A screened deck out back makes for pleasant early evening sipping in summer.

▼ ▼ ▼ ▼ ▼ ▼ ▼ ▼ ▼ ▼ ▼ ▼ ▼ ▼ ▼ ▼ ▼ ▼

La Pointe

Tom's Burned Down Cafe
Highway H
(715) 747-6100

I f one were to construct the mythic archetype of the Northwoods tavern, with all the eccentric ties that can be found in the land of pines and lakes, and roll them into a ball that is at once edgy and laid-back, well, you'd probably have something approximating Tom's Burned Down Cafe. It's worth checking out on your next Bayfield/Madeline Island trip and can be driven to only via the Madeline Island Ferry. Hey, if you're in the neighborhood there's no good reason not to visit Madeline Island.

When you arrive, you can ask the questions I would have liked to have answered here. The story behind the name? I heard four distinct versions, but there's definitely a fire in there somewhere. What do they have to drink? Heard several answers to that one, too: depends, whatever we've got, and whatever we remembered to order. When are they open? Take your pick: 11 A.M. to 2 A.M., 4 P.M. to 10 P.M., or when they get around to it.

Readers have probably noticed that I find taverns to be excellent places to swap stories. Well, Tom's holds its own on that score. What is more unusual is the number of stories about Tom's. It is not uncommon to hear tales about Tom's in the far reaches of the other quadrants of Wisconsin. Beer drinker/explorers in Blue Mounds, Okee, Coon Valley, and Cedarburg have related lore about this island tavern. Some of the stories are humorous, some outrageous, and others mysterious. Some think the stories relate to the mythic quality of the quest to find the place open.

Another draw for Tom's is the fiction that one can be a celebrity (or at least a celebrity in one's mind) and visit incognito without detection. Thus some public figures periodically don fishing vests and floppy hats and smugly sip in the belief that their disguises have fooled the masses. No way. It's just that nobody at Tom's gives a damn about those who are legends in their own minds.

Don't drive 300 miles thinking you'll just drop in. Call from home, call from halfway there, and call from Bayfield before you get on the ferry. You may get Tom's message, "I'm either out of town or so close to it, it's almost the same thing." Not to worry, the joke's not on you. No trip to this part of God's country is wasted.

Menominee

The Buck
315 Main Street
(715) 235-9390

A play on words creates lighthearted confusion at the site of the Silver Dollar Saloon and Brick Company. "The Buck" was appended to the bar area of this business as shorthand for the basic unit of U.S. currency. The overall establishment and dining area are given the longer appellation. This is a favorite spot for tavern lovers in northwest Wisconsin. When you ask the sales reps and beer distributors in the area which bar they like, many shoot back "the Buck" as fast as a pool table break shot.

A classic rock CD collection (with plenty of Eric Clapton) keeps the Buck at a high energy level. If you have a hankering for a sandwich or dinner, you might want to relocate to the dining areas. The food is well regarded by some of my trustier sources. On Friday afternoons there is a pleasant Cheers-type ambience. A healthy mix of UW-Stout students, downtown professionals, and blue-collar beer purists are drawn by the 20 import beers and Guinness and New Glarus brews on tap. The full Leinie's line finds favor here, with Leinenkugel's Creamy Draft filling a comfortable niche. The Buck's Bloody Mary is a favorite in Menominee.

Many taverns sponsor sports teams. More than a few take pride in those teams and the trophies they bring home to roost behind the bar. These sports enthusiasts take a backseat to no one in that regard, with team spirit that extends year-round. The crowd at the Buck takes this competitive spirit a step further with a widely appreciated cheerleading squad.

This crowd also excels in another area: that of Minnesota humor. Well, some of it is humor. Some of it must be labeled as creative insult. A tinier category might fall within the realm of defamation if those stolid Minnesotans were prone to litigation. On my last visit the barrage was directed at Vikings, Gophers, and the Mall of America. Where Garrison Keillor uses the wry approach, Buck denizens use wisecracking smart bombs.

▼ ▼ ▼ ▼ ▼ ▼ ▼ ▼ ▼ ▼ ▼ ▼ ▼ ▼ ▼ ▼ ▼

Minong
Fluffy's Corner Bar
203 Fifth Avenue
(715) 466-4318

Fluffy's was a totally accidental find. Visits to other area taverns brought warnings to avoid Fluffy's and vague complaints about "that wild place" from elderly patrons of more sedate spots. The red flags, of course, whetted my desire to check it out.

What I found was part Northwoods tavern, part Harley-Davidson biker bar, and part town hall. During the day it's pretty much a family place. By evening it's decidedly adult. Delicate souls are forewarned about off-color signs and "art." Meat Loaf seems to be a favorite on the jukebox. Customers sometimes yell conversations down the length of the bar. But you know, it's a friendly place. It's the tavern equivalent of a well-broken-in work boot: scuffed and not much to look at, but comfortable as all get-out.

No one knows for sure what beers are available in Fluffy's. It seems to depend on who asks. Sure, the standard brands are all represented. But the quick eye will pick up furtive bartender moves to pluck Guinness Stout, Heineken, and other unheralded exotic fare from the cooler depths. One patron offered the theory that any beer sold in Big Betty's Bottle Shop, an adjoining business connected by a low doorway, might show up in Fluffy's. My companion and I tested the proposition and found a bit of sweet talk did indeed produce results.

The sociology of Big Betty's Bottle Shop makes for interesting exchanges shouted through the doorway into Fluffy's. As far as I can tell, there must be a segment of the liquor store's patrons who choose not to cross the threshold for one reason or another (though a few have the banned-for-life look). Instead they choose to hurl insults and unsolicited lame jokes through the doorway.

Fluffy's has its share of physically imposing customers, often in leather with Harley logos. Yet they are full of pleasant surprises, as I found when one grizzled biker made an on-the-money referral to a great prime rib supper club and allowed that the red meat was accompanied by the Northwoods' best cabernet list. But he was one of those quirky types that show up in places like this—filled with Beat generation literary references and spouting quotes from the works of eco-renegade Edward Abbey.

▼ ▼ ▼ ▼ ▼ ▼ ▼ ▼ ▼ ▼ ▼ ▼ ▼ ▼ ▼ ▼ ▼ ▼ ▼

ANOTHER ROUND
Some Wisconsin Beer Facts

First Commercial Brewery: Phillips Brewery in Mineral Point, founded in 1835. This business evolved into the Mineral Springs Brewery, which continued brewing until 1961. Wisconsin's second brewery, Rablin & Bray, opened in 1836 in an abandoned Black Hawk War log fort at Elk Grove, Lafayette County.

Most Durable Brewery: Joseph Huber in Monroe. Despite many restructurings and name changes, this brewery traces its roots back to 1848. It continues to offer beer under the Huber and Berghoff labels.

Old and New Styles: G. Heileman's initial main brand was Gold Leaf Beer. It was replaced in 1902 by Old Style Lager. The new brew acquired an excellent word-of-mouth reputation. In 1933, when Prohibition was repealed, the reopened brewery worked around the clock to fill back orders from places as distant as Los Angeles and the West Indies. A riot nearly broke out when caravans of truckers descended on La Crosse and refused to leave town without full loads of beer.

▼ ▼ ▼ ▼ ▼ ▼ ▼ ▼ ▼ ▼ ▼ ▼ ▼ ▼ ▼ ▼

Neillsville
Green Lantern
231 W. Seventh Street
(715) 743-3663

Neillsville is one of those towns where one of its eight or nine taverns always seems to be reopening, shutting down, or changing hands. Tavern culture is lively here (much like Ridgeway and Hollandale down in my Iowa County turf) and reminiscent of the old-fashioned shot-and-a-beer ethic. Several of the local spots are high-octane testosterone bars, featuring nude calendars and (mostly) good-natured profanity.

Such tavern-blessed towns usually have at least one bar that takes a lower-key approach. But nearly 20 years of stopping in Neillsville for a quick one (OK, a quick two) kept me in a one- or two-block area of reliable (as in open for business) taverns. Then came the revelation. It came in strange form, too, for someone accustomed to hearing tales in tavern settings. Instead, I went to a sacred place to hear a strange tale and as a bonus was steered to an unassuming place called the Green Lanern.

The Green Lantern stands apart from the other bars, a bit quieter and more reflective, and set off a bit from the main tavern cluster. It is not uncommon to run into visitors and staff from the Highground, Wisconsin's Vietnam Veterans Memorial. Don't worry, you won't be a captive audience for someone else's war stories. But you just might get to eavesdrop on middle-aged men in fatigues whispering about a youth spent in a faraway land. On rainy days campers and fishermen stop by to dry out, wet the whistle, and plug a jukebox that carries polkas and Jim Morrison.

Simplicity is the password here, with only two beer taps—both Old Milwaukee. Cans and bottles: if it's not Miller or Old Style, it's exotic. Liquor: only what regular customers ask for (and don't expect anything with fruit or tiny umbrellas). Food: burger, fish sandwich, chicken sandwich, and fish fry ($4.25!). Be nice to Rosie behind the bar and she might give you a bowl of peanuts in the shell. If you're up after the big buck, she can also get you a range pass for the Neillsville Gun Club.

▼ ▼ ▼ ▼ ▼ ▼ ▼ ▼ ▼ ▼ ▼ ▼ ▼ ▼ ▼ ▼ ▼ ▼ ▼

River Falls

Main Streeter Bar and Grill
212 S. Main Street
(715) 425-2202

Here's a watering hole with a brand-spanking-new look that nevertheless possesses character and holds a crowd of regulars. This is one of the most family-friendly taverns I encountered in my travels. Plenty of video games for the kids and an endless supply of popcorn. The Main Streeter is a favorite of parents visiting UW–River Falls and also picks up quite a few day-trippers from Minnesota. All mingle at the bar and exchange sports talk and local news. The place has a pleasant buzz and smiling faces, not the high-decibel roar or the sullen silence that you find in some spots.

Ten taps tell the tale of draft beer for thirsty crowds, with Leinie's, the nationals, and Pete's Wicked Ale. The coolers usually hold 25 different bottled beers, including the full Leinie's line and a few rarities like Newcastle Brown Ale. If you hit the place at the right time you're likely to hear young faculty arguing with gray-templed carpenters about macrobrews versus microbrews. The surprise is in who takes which side.

A diverse crowd hints at the Main Streeter's triple duty as sports bar, downtown lunch spot, and 30-something meeting place. The menu bucks Wisconsin tradition by not offering a fish fry. The top food item is a very good half-pound burger. Regular patrons also vouch for the other sandwiches and daily specials. It's a testament to the atmosphere and offerings that so many travelers become repeat customers. One elderly woman from Eau Claire told me this is one of only three taverns she would set foot in.

The Main Streeter probably represents a sturdy middle ground for the taverns of the future, outside of the emerging franchise operations. Not all will be able to go glitzy, pull in the bands, or set up brewing operations. Some, like this one, will carve out a niche as modernized family taverns that make everyone feel welcome.

▼ ▼ ▼ ▼ ▼ ▼ ▼ ▼ ▼ ▼ ▼ ▼ ▼ ▼ ▼ ▼ ▼ ▼

Solon Springs
Village Pump
11575 South Business 53
(715) 378-2212

This is the party spot for the surrounding area. Even on a Saturday night you might well end up in the middle of someone's birthday celebration, anniversary party, or wedding reception (I put $5 in a pitcher to dance with a new bride). The large, open lodge-style construction makes this one of the biggest tavern venues north of Eau Claire. A long bar means that there is rarely a stool shortage.

Regular customers like their draft beer, even though the four tap selections are limited to standard national brands. Leinie's and a few imports are available in bottles. Local quirks include demand for Busch Light in bottles and Leinie's in cans. The regulars also go through a lot of brandy. One trusty source told me that at least one segment of the crowd here likes to play drinking games, though that pursuit seemed to be the province of the younger folks.

The regulars like to shoot pool and play cards. During one visit I ran into a wedding rehearsal party, and the bride was shooting pool with her veil on. We were told that they host quite a few bachelor and bachelorette parties where the revelers shoot pool throughout the event, except when one of the participants ends up dancing on the table. As with many small-town events, the general public is welcome, no matter if the occasion is Johnny's welcome back from boot camp or Grandma and Grandpa's anniversary.

The Village Pump is geared mainly to the younger, active crowd. There is a high turnover at the bar stools, with 20-somethings in and out for quick burgers and beer. So it's not a place for prolonged conversation, but you can catch the buzz about what's going on locally and track down the four-season recreational opportunities that abound in the area. The jukebox is well stocked and people dance to it, even to sad Patsy Cline numbers.

Some would say that the Village Pump represents an updating of the roadhouse-style tavern, and they'd be part right. The layout is reminiscent of many roadhouse variations and certainly holds its own on floor space with the heftier representatives of that species. What is different is the brighter and airier interior and the clearer demarcations between the spaces devoted to different recreational purposes. It took a bit of getting used to, but I can now see that they planned wisely. They just might have come up with a new model.

▼ ▼ ▼ ▼ ▼ ▼ ▼ ▼ ▼ ▼ ▼ ▼ ▼ ▼ ▼ ▼ ▼ ▼

Spooner

Hogs Head Saloon
110 South River Street
(715) 635-8885

Football fans in northwest Wisconsin tell me that this bar is the demilitarized zone for the rivalry between the Green Bay Packers and the Minnesota Vikings. One TV screen (the smaller one) is devoted to Vikings games. Another screen (the larger one) is devoted to Packers games. The rivalry in this town between the fans of the respective teams is heated, loud, and longstanding. So far, law enforcement intervention has not been needed. But a bartender here needs some mediation skills.

The verbal sparks fly when the two NFC Central Division teams meet for their fall clashes. Perhaps more interesting for the football purists are the recounted memories of past games recited by some of the regulars. As my band of roving sports and beer enthusiasts found out on our last stop, the tales go back to the days of leather helmets and Curly Lambeau.

The Hogs Head is a split-level bar that shares a building with a sporting goods store. The two establishments seem to bring business to each other. Some may remember this bar as Patrick's. Mike Mills, co-owner with wife Therisa, is a Union Pacific (formerly Chicago and Northwestern) railroad employee and used the train slang for engineer to rechristen his new fueling spot. But a mounted hog's head on the wall lends double meaning to the name. And, I might add, the rail connection makes for some mighty fine accounts of the latter-day travails of that industry when Mike's buddies drop in.

No tap beer here. Customer requests run heavily toward Leinie's and Old Milwaukee. Summer brings a younger crowd to Margarita Wednesdays on an outdoor party deck. Winter brings an older crowd of snowmobilers in off the nearby trail for schnapps and brandy. But Fridays and Saturdays produce a mixed-age crowd that includes DNR employees, trainmen, woods workers, and construction tradespeople. All give Therisa high grades for holding down the fort on days when Mike is on the rails. The couple is regarded as one of the friendliest husband-and-wife teams in the tavern business. Such kind words are spoken about them from Danbury to Bloomer.

▼ ▼ ▼ ▼ ▼ ▼ ▼ ▼ ▼ ▼ ▼ ▼ ▼ ▼ ▼ ▼ ▼

St. Croix Falls

Kassel Tap Bar
Highways 8 and 35 North
(715) 483-9390

Kassel's, as many of the locals refer to it, has been in its current incarnation for about 15 years. Because a number of predecessor bars operated on this site, there are three and four generations of some outdoors families with a tradition of using this spot as a way station for their trips "up north." One of the best things that can happen to a first-time visitor is for one of the elderly gentlemen who still drop in here to regale them with his memories of fishing and hunting trips his father took him on and how those trips included a boy's first tavern visit.

Memories of rites of passage hang as thick around the white heads of those old-timers as smoke from a pipe. First muskie caught on a hand-carved lure. First overnight canoe passage on an isolated flowage in a custom-crafted cedar canoe. First big buck in a camp of skilled hunters who had waited decades for a trophy. First beer in a bar with Dad and the uncles. So at its best, Kassel's is primed for memories of the Wisconsin that no longer exists.

But don't tell that to the regulars. Many of them consider it a combination outdoorsmen's and sports bar. It's considered the local spot to catch big games on the bar TV. Locals, hunters, fishermen, and vacationers mingle here. In summers, softball teams stop by to quench their thirst while volleyball teams work up a thirst on the courts out back. Road construction crews also seem to be among the perennial visitors.

The three taps and bottled beers are limited to the standard nationals and Northwoods regionals, which is just fine for the blue-collar regulars. Others opt for the hot beef sandwiches and pickled asparagus (sold in jars to go as well). Polk County friends swear that Kassel Tap is the political and social barometer for the area, with frequent animated conversations on land use topics. When they're talking politics in here, they're talking conservation from the pre–ecology movement perspective.

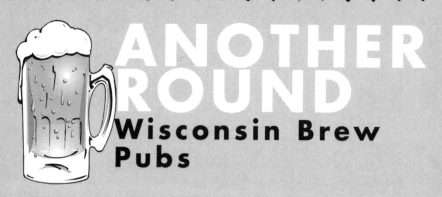

ANOTHER ROUND
Wisconsin Brew Pubs

Be sure to call ahead for the hours each is open.

Angelic Brewing Company
322 West Johnson Street
Madison
(608) 257-2707
www.angelicbrewing.com

Appleton Brewing Company
1004 S. Olde Oneida Street
Appleton
(920) 731-3322

Brewery Creek Inn and Pub
23 Commerce Street
Mineral Point
(608) 987-3298
www.brewerycreek.com
(See page 63 for full description.)

Brewmasters Brew Pub and Brewmasters Northside
4017 80th Street and 1170 22nd Avenue
Kenosha
(262) 694-9050 and (262) 552-2085
(See page 15 for full description.)

Brown Street Brewery
16 North Brown Street
Rhinelander
(715) 369-2100

Delafield Brewhaus
3832 Hillside Drive
Delafield
(262) 646-7821

▼ ▼ ▼ ▼ ▼ ▼ ▼ ▼ ▼ ▼ ▼ ▼ ▼ ▼ ▼ ▼ ▼ ▼ ▼

Egan Brewing Company
330 Reid Street
De Pere
(920) 339-2707

Endehouse Brewery and Restaurant
1020 E. Main Street
Reedsburg
(608) 524-8600
(See page 74 for full description.)

Fox River Brewing Company
1501 Arboretum Drive
Oshkosh
(920) 232-2337

Fox River Brewing Company (No. 2)
4301 Wisconsin Avenue
Appleton
(920) 991-0000

Great Dane Pub and Brewing Company
123 E. Doty Street
Madison
(608) 284-0000
www.greatdanepub.com

Isadore Street Brewery
200 Isadore Street
Stevens Point
(715) 341-1199
(See page 123 for full description.)

J. T. Whitney's Brewpub
674 S. Whitney Way
Madison
(608) 274-1776
www.jtwhitneys.com

Milwaukee Ale House
233 N. Water Street
Milwaukee
(414) 226-2337
www.ale-house.com
(See page 31 for full description.)

Minocqua Brewing Company
238 Lake Shore Drive
Minocqua
(715) 358-3040
www.minocquabrewingco.com

Mount Horeb Pub and Brewery
105 S. Second Street
Mount Horeb
(608) 437-4200

Northwoods Brew Pub and Grill
3560 Oakwood Mall Drive
Eau Claire
(715) 552-0511
www.northwoodsbrewpub.com
(See page 85 for full description.)

Port Washington Brewing Company
100 N. Franklin Street
Port Washington
(262) 377-2337

Pumphouse Pizza
19 W. Monroe Street
Lake Delton
(608) 253-4687

Rail House Brewing Company
2029 W. Old Peshtigo Road
Marinette
(715) 735-9800
(See page 114 for full description.)

Randy's Fun Hunters Brewery
841 E. Milwaukee Street
Whitewater
(262) 473-8000
(See page 49 for full description.)

Rock Bottom Brewery
740 N. Plankinton Road
Milwaukee
(414) 276-3030

Rothaus
4900 Highway 175
Hartford (St. Lawrence)
(262) 644-8181
(See page 13 for full description.)

Rowland's Calumet Brewing Company
25 N. Madison Street
Chilton
(920) 849-2534
(See page 6 for full description.)

▼ ▼ ▼ ▼ ▼ ▼ ▼ ▼ ▼ ▼ ▼ ▼ ▼ ▼ ▼ ▼ ▼ ▼

Shipwrecked Brewpub
7791 Egg Harbor Road
Egg Harbor
(920) 868-2767

South Shore Brewery
400 Third Avenue West
Ashland
(715) 682-9199

Sturgeon Bay Brewery
341 N. Third Avenue
Sturgeon Bay
(920) 746-7611

Titletown Brewery
200 Douseman Street
Green Bay
(920) 437-2337
www.titletownbrewery.com

Water Street Brewery
1101 N. Water Street
Milwaukee
(414) 272-1195
www.restaurantour.com/wsb
(See page 34 for full description.)

▼ ▼ ▼ ▼ ▼ ▼ ▼ ▼ ▼ ▼ ▼ ▼ ▼ ▼ ▼ ▼ ▼ ▼

Superior

Anchor Bar and Grill
413 Tower Avenue
(715) 394-9747

Not much to look at from the outside, and located in a gritty warehouse neighborhood, "Da Anchor" (as many locals refer to it) is a delight to enter and survey. My referral source spoke of its "maritime look" and conjured up an image of tavern à la Red Lobster. What a misimpression!

The interior could be the cove-side cottage of an old salt. It is as if a massive northeaster blew all the flotsam and jetsam between Nova Scotia and Isle Royale right through the Anchor's front door. The result is an eclectic but warm beachcomber's clutter. The late-Saturday-night crowd I found there was an appropriate mix of blue-collar, white-collar, students, and down-and-outers, with a sprinkling of merchant seamen.

If you are alone you might be able to find a stool at the short (and usually crowded) bar and pick up on a lively conversation. A weathered old chap told me an eerie haunted lighthouse tale. He put a whole new light on the sweeping beam that peeked through the motor home's windows later that night.

This is the type of place where you don't really need a local character to tell you a story. Da Anchor births them and inspires them. A few hours on the stools and a landlocked flatlander will be spinning yarns before the mast. Good company, heads nodding in encouragement, and good beer see to that. B. Traven, early-twentieth-century writer of a haunting and scathing maritime novel called *Death Ship*, would blend right in here.

But if you are part of a group—especially a hungry group—you are well advised to claim a worn wooden table in one of the book-lined alcoves. While my arrival was not well timed to test the kitchen's mettle, patrons made sure that I knew that *Northland Reader* of Duluth, Minnesota, gave the Anchor its 1998 "Best Really Cheap Eats" award for the Lake Superior country. Hearty and ample characterize the testimonials of regulars I talked to.

The Anchor is the best of a covey of other small but interesting bars in this commercial area. What sets it apart (aside from atmosphere and grub) are the beers. It has a growing collection of bottled micros (15). Space limits it to three tap heads, with a regional and a micro in the rotation. We lucked out with a Lake Superior India Pale Ale.

Northeast Wisconsin

▼ ▼ ▼ ▼ ▼ ▼ ▼ ▼ ▼ ▼ ▼ ▼ ▼ ▼ ▼ ▼ ▼ ▼

This diverse area presents many faces, moods, and settings. It is home to isolated lake and loon country and some of Wisconsin's worst sprawl. It is potato farming, forest products, and papermaking. It is prosperity, skilled industrial workers, real estate speculation, and rural poverty. It is an ethnic stew where the original Menominee, Potawatomi, and Ojibwa were joined by French, New England Yankees, displaced eastern tribes, Belgians, Bohemians, Icelanders, Danes, Dutch, Poles, Finns, Norwegians, Swedes, and Germans.

This quadrant of Wisconsin slices across several bioregions and economic clusters. Door County has much in common with the smaller Lake Michigan shore communities stretching into the southeast. Green Bay and Appleton are logically part of the urban belt in the Fox Valley. Sections of national forest lands are indistinguishable from adjacent tracts in the northwest. And while the northeast claims a large chunk of the central sands country, the ancient lake bottom is really part of all four quadrants of the state.

Socially and politically, this is Wisconsin's most conservative region. But it has little of the "dry" tradition of southwest Wisconsin. The landscape is dotted with Catholic and Lutheran churches, often at crossroads with a tavern. The urban portions are noted for hardworking early risers, yet one readily notices more strip joints, in the form of "gentlemen's clubs," than elsewhere in the state.

It is the part of Wisconsin most content to constantly reinvent itself. Despite a proud history that reaches back to the French explorers, the taverns are generally not historic buildings. Some say that the forests in the Northwoods portion, like Yucatan jungles, devour the isolated taverns. In the urban area, bulldozers clean the slate of old neighborhoods and factories to make way for malls. Franchise and chain pubs prove to be very popular.

Still, there are many worthy taverns in the northeast. Backroad searches turn up hidden gems. Resort areas are joining the brew pub and microbrew trend. The cities have many unheralded neighborhood taverns that are 100% pure cheesehead territory. Part of the fun is finding your own favorites and telling other people about them.

▼ ▼ ▼ ▼ ▼ ▼ ▼ ▼ ▼ ▼ ▼ ▼ ▼ ▼ ▼ ▼ ▼

Algoma

Hudson's Bar and Grill
205 Navarino Street
(920) 487-5493

Hudson's is set up more like a supper club than a bar and grill. Yet it earns the right to belong to the tavern fraternity by providing a comfortable bar and bartenders who treat their domain as more than a brief stop for patrons on the way to the dining area. It also provides one of the great tavern experiences of the Lake Michigan shoreline.

Two short blocks from the lake, gulls often circle nearby. Many customers stroll up from the Algoma boardwalk. Others stop in after tours of the nearby Von Stiehl Winery. In the warmer months it is an ideal place to catch up with the latest lake fishing reports. My introduction to Hudson's came through friends who routinely bring their lake trout and salmon fishing gangs to tell lies after their charter trips.

The taps are from the ranks of the standard nationals, but the bottled selection usually includes regional craft brews. If you like fish with your beer, you're in luck: seaburger, perchburger (a treat), cod, redfish, whitefish, rainbow trout, haddock, pollock, and the local favorite, lake perch. Steaks and hamburgers are available for landlubbers.

Hudson's is also a hit with retired patrons. Many taverns have displaced elderly customers with loud music, foul language, and rowdy 20-somethings chugging six-packs. Management here seems to have come down on the side of the more mature beer drinker and multigenerational family groups that come in for food. Some tavern owners say that such a business can't survive. In Algoma it thrives.

From the Wisconsin heritage perspective, this spot also scores points with those who wish to hear lake yarns, especially about the old sailing-ship days. In each one of my three visits I picked up tales of shipwrecks, lost sailors, and haunted lighthouses. There are, of course, lighthearted stories to be told, too. My favorite was about the old bawdy house that flew various undergarments from its tall flagpole as a signal to passing vessels about which working gals were on duty.

That tale brought denials from women patrons that any such institution had plied sordid trades in Algoma. A grizzled boat repairman said he heard it from his sainted grandfather. Who would argue with that?

▼ ▼ ▼ ▼ ▼ ▼ ▼ ▼ ▼ ▼ ▼ ▼ ▼ ▼ ▼ ▼ ▼ ▼

Appleton

Adler Brau Restaurant and Pub

1004 South Olde Oneida Street

(920) 380-BEER

Here's the online and on-site alternative to mail order beer clubs. It pulls loyal locals and travelers in to sample from 12 award-winning brews produced on the premises. Then it sets customers up to order via the internet. Email them at appbrau@vbe.com and they'll zip back an order form.

The restaurant side of the establishment also gets good reviews. The menu presents numerous choices with its American, German, Italian, and Mexican specialties. The building is almost as old as the state and started as—surprise, surprise—a brewery. This is an excellent alternative to the student hustle and bustle on College Avenue.

The place gets my vote as the best watering hole in Appleton for good conversation, especially if your interests range beyond the Packers. Not that they don't talk sports here; you'll even encounter fans of minor league baseball reliving the feats of the boys of summer. What is more astounding is that you might even hear a rational political discussion here. Elsewhere in town there are those who toast Tailgunner Joe McCarthy and speculate on the positive nutritional value of PCBs.

This brew spot is also to be commended for its bucking of Fox Valley trends toward the strip malling of all cultural institutions. Yes, there is value in preservation. Yes, beer can be joyfully consumed without high-volume TV accompaniment. Yes, there is life after 30.

▼ ▼ ▼ ▼ ▼ ▼ ▼ ▼ ▼ ▼ ▼ ▼ ▼ ▼ ▼

Appleton
Bazil's Pub
109 West College Avenue
(920) 954-1707

Appleton's College Avenue is one of Wisconsin's longest bar strips. Many fine drinking establishments line this heavily commercial thoroughfare. They range from the bars of the young, upscale downtown crowd to the blue-collar shot joints further west. Bazil's Pub bridges those two worlds with a large beer collection.

This party hearty location runs ten taps. It does something different with its taps than most microbrew bars. Instead of going for a variety of brands from different breweries, it'll often run a featured brewery and offer most, if not all, of the available brews from that source. It might offer four or five Gray's at a time, or the local Adler Brau line.

The bottled beer inventory is in the 100 brew range, with heavy import and micro representation. Bazil's also has an extensive menu, with good sandwiches and variations on the usual fried appetizers, like calamari. The diverse crowd also has better gender balance than in most bars. The women regulars appreciate the less-male-dominated atmosphere and the clean facilities.

It's an all-around decent place for any part of the day or any day of the week. Despite its catering to a crowd in their 20s and 30s, those of us in the neighborhood of the big 5-0 are not made to feel like lepers. Service is excellent for a casual dining and drinking spot. Elsewhere on College Avenue the hired help can run toward the sassy side and the bartenders know more about flushing beer than tapping it.

Mere niceness rarely elevates a pub into respectable beer-drinking territory, but it sure doesn't hurt when you have the other qualities that bring people into Bazil's. It's a place that knows how to keep them coming back.

If Bazil's is insufficiently gritty for you, just work your way west on College Avenue. Eventually you'll happen upon the American Legion Club. If the moon is full you just might hear a strange Joe McCarthy story.

▼ ▼ ▼ ▼ ▼ ▼ ▼ ▼ ▼ ▼ ▼ ▼ ▼ ▼ ▼ ▼ ▼ ▼

Boulder Junction

Boulder Beer Bar
Highway K and Main Street
(715) 385-2749

Many Wisconsin taverns lay claim to having the most beers available for sale. Behind the inflated rhetoric, inquiring customers hear a lot of "We're temporarily out of . . ." or "The day person must have moved our . . ." You won't hear these excuses at the Boulder Beer Bar. At last count it was at 384 types of bottled beer. Its goal is 500. By all indications it satisfies its claims and will meet its target.

The full line of Wisconsin microbrews from New Glarus, Hinterland, and Wisconsin Brewing are available. All the other Badger State microbreweries are represented by their generally distributed brews. Dozens and dozens of American microbrews also grace the coolers of the Boulder Beer Bar. So do dozens and dozens of quality imports. For example, they carry seven Belgian brews. Europe is very well represented, as are all the other continents with breweries.

One problem associated with a wide selection (aside from bogus claims) is stale and skunky beer. Even bars in large metropolitan areas have slow turnover among more obscure brews. Boulder Beer Bar works to control such difficulties by maintaining small-quantity inventories with a computer system that prompts constant fresh orders.

Boulder Beer Bar is also one of the state's leading snowmobiler bars. It is conveniently located near the heart of the Minoqua–Boulder Junction network of hundreds of miles of snowmobile trails. It is a very lively place in January and February if the white stuff is on the trails. But it's definitely worth a stop in any season. Call ahead for hours. They close some weekdays.

This probably is as good a time as any to figuratively shake the collars of all those sourpusses who possess tavern licenses in this beautiful but beer-deprived corner of Wisconsin. Visit the Boulder Beer Bar! See customers with functioning pulses! Learn that there is more to beer slinging than Schiltz and Pabst! If we can elevate those dreary little wayside bars, with their depressing interiors that draw more on the tradition of the tarpaper shack than the Northwoods lodge, to one-tenth of the ambition of the Boulder Beer Bar, well, we will have ourselves a renaissance.

▼ ▼ ▼ ▼ ▼ ▼ ▼ ▼ ▼ ▼ ▼ ▼ ▼ ▼ ▼ ▼ ▼ ▼

Starlight Bar (in the North Star Casino)
Hwy A
(715) 787-3110

D rinking beer or other alcoholic beverages is not what brings most patrons into the complex owned and operated by the Mohican band of Stockbridge-Munsee in northwest Shawano County. But unlike a lot of casino bars, this bar holds its own in business. Sometimes it's like its own little community within the casino. Casino crowds are weighted heavily toward seniors, but here at the bar is where you're most likely to meet people who are not members of AARP.

The bar is a bit hard to find in the casino, so wander toward the big blue "Keno-Progressive" sign. Each bar stool location has a flat in the bar surface draw poker video machine. The players are often intense, and you are advised not to chatter with those so engrossed. The bartenders are friendly but careful not to interrupt play. They are also, as is a Native American custom, extremely solicitous of senior citizens.

The main drawback here is the cacaphony of the nearby slots. The action is hot and heavy, and the sound effects make you feel like you're sitting near a calliope. I'm just a sucker (and I telegraph my Pennsylvania heritage in the process) for any Northwoods spot that runs specials on Rolling Rock.

If you're lucky enough to arrive at an off time and there's a Stockbridge tribal member behind the bar, you just might get to hear a few Munsee/Mohican legends. The tribe has an interesting history, with story traditions that trace back to New England and the mid-Atlantic states. See if you can get anyone to talk of the Ohdohs, a ghost tribe that some say followed the Mohicans on their trail of travails. Or you might hear a story about the American Revolution; the Stockbridge reservation has more descendants of that hallowed war for indepedence than any other Native American community of its size west of the Appalachians.

DePere

Egan Brewing Company
330 Reid Street
(920) 339-2707

Here the sequence of business development followed an unusual pattern. Egan's started out as a brewery, then added a bar, and finally added a restaurant side of the business. It was a commonsense approach that allowed the staff and management to build skills and avoid some of the growth pangs that other brew pubs experience. The result is an excellent combination of beer, food, and hospitality.

The brewing here walks on the wild side with Wilsteraner Altbier, Raspberry Ginger Mead, Princess of Darkness Porter, nitro-poured stout, Doppelbock, and Abbot Pennings Belgian trippel. Brew pub standards like traditional ale, brown ale, pale ale, honey ale, Oktoberfest, and hefe weizen are also available. Fox Valley beer tasters have kind words for all of them. The altbier tickled my fancy on my first visit. When I returned the porter had been upped a notch and can be commended as top-shelf.

The dining area is also top-shelf. An ambitious menu and generous servings impress those who put dining before imbibing. The chicken chili is a big hit and the pasta and beef dishes satisfy big appetites. From top to bottom, Egan's tries hard to please and succeeds. On Friday night, as in much of Wisconsin, there is a bit of a wait. But the lightly breaded perch is worth it (and presents the perfect opportunity to use your time wisely by reconnoitering the sample tray of available brews, which is reason enough to work a designated driver into your visit plans).

Only one note of caution must be raised for the traveler: finding Egan's. The task of navigation is a bit convoluted if you're starting from the downtown Green Bay hotels. A work colleague and I had to make four stops for directions on our first foray. The first three convenience store clerks had never heard of it. The young women at a liquor store five blocks away had never heard of it! Fortunately, a beer-savvy customer in the store came to my rescue. My advice: chart your course on a local street map.

Even when you arrive, you're not sure you're in the right place. Likely as not, you'll approach via a looping street, pass some railroad tracks, and come upon some strip mall shops punctuated by older buildings. Not to worry, the decor and mood inside are definitely not strip mall. Surprisingly, there are a few other decent bars in the area.

▼ ▼ ▼ ▼ ▼ ▼ ▼ ▼ ▼ ▼ ▼ ▼ ▼ ▼ ▼ ▼

Green Bay
Cock & Bull Publick House
1237 Main Street
(920) 432-1885

The C and B is a Main Street institution in Green Bay. Main Street is the rough equivalent of Madison's State Street or Milwaukee's Water Street. Out-of-towners start in this neighborhood because of its proximity to the downtown hotels and conference centers.

A few words about Main Street. It is an eclectic collection of generally youthful bars, pizza parlors, strip clubs, coffeehouses, shot-and-beer joints, at least one Latin music club, and a bar for alternative scenes. Many consider the C and B the crown jewel of the street.

While we are at it, mention should also be made of Green Bay's fragmented and evolving tavern scene. Broadway at one time had a solid six blocks of bars, but these were hit hard by urban renewal. Neighborhood bars are widely dispersed. The "downtown" is more the province of hotel/motel lounges. So Main Street is your best bet for a compact pub crawl.

The C and B is a spacious establishment with a well-appointed bar, an abundance of pool tables, and a design that encourages mingling. The look is a combination of traditional tavern flavor with brassier modern club elements. It is often crowded, especially on Friday and Saturday nights. Despite the heavy traffic, this nightspot is well kept and the service is prompt.

Its ads boast a beer list of over 200 selections, but the posting on brands is not always clear, and it could use some compact printed lists throughout the bar area. About eight taps are rotated on a seasonal basis. The current favorites are the home team selections from Hinterland. That brewery's Pub Draft, served up through this bar's nitrogen-charged tap, is as creamy a malt concoction as can be found this side of a root beer float. C and B's is one of the leading purveyors of this beer. It also stocks a collection of top-shelf liquor.

The ambience here is upscale pool hall, with multiple tables in action and an abundance of players. A warning to the guys: don't assume that you're going to teach the gals here your cue and table moves. There are some good women pool players here and you just might get hustled.

▼ ▼ ▼ ▼ ▼ ▼ ▼ ▼ ▼ ▼ ▼ ▼ ▼ ▼ ▼ ▼ ▼ ▼ ▼

ANOTHER ROUND

Beer- and Tavern-Related Websites

75,000 pages about beer: www.realbeer.com

Canadian beer festivals: www.cottagecreekevents.com

European brewery tours: www.kiss.com/fr/mir/EBA.html

General beer guide: www.allaboutbeer.com

General beer information, including bar tips, secret hangover cures, humor, drink recipes, bar operations, etiquette: www.thevirtualbar.com

Guide to exotic and specialty beers: www.beerhunter.com

Guide to pubs, including 2,000 North American sites: www.beerexpedition.com

Home brewing supplies:

At Home Warehouse Distributors: www.ahwd.com

Brewfellows: www.brewfellows.com

Northern Brewery: www.nbrewer.com

Williams Brewing: www.williamsbrewing.com

Milwaukee/Southeast Wisconsin beer news: www.creamcitysuds.com

National pub crawl network: www.pubcrawler.com

Roadmap guides to microbreweries and brew pubs: www.coopsmaps.com

U.S. brewery listings, with Wisconsin section: www.beertown.org

Wisconsin beer page: www.geocities.com/CollegePark/Union/4491/beer.html

▼ ▼ ▼ ▼ ▼ ▼ ▼ ▼ ▼ ▼ ▼ ▼ ▼ ▼ ▼ ▼ ▼

Keshena

War Bonnet
Highway 47 and 55
(715) 799-4335

Nestled on the southern edge of the internationally renowned Menominee reservation forest and a stone's throw from the Wolf River, the War Bonnet is one of the few pit stops along the Wolf. The ambience combines the country-and-western feel common in rural bars with the local tribal culture. You won't find many other spots where a lively discussion about the Crandon mine and water quality can rage among half the patrons while the other half watch *Dukes of Hazard* reruns. However, if you feel the need to debate treaty rights, spearfishing, and the virtues of Christopher Columbus, this is not the spot for you.

This is a true reservation bar as one might experience out west, not a tourist and trinket stop. Wisconsin reservations do not have many bars, and tribal elders often raise objections to alcohol consumption. This means that you need to value the atmosphere and not crave amenities. Standard national beers and a few regionals wet the whistles of loggers and fishermen. Thursday night is dollar night and weekends bring DJs and bands.

Though short on my favorite brews, the Bonnet is well stocked on Northwoods lore. A good story requires that the listeners buy a round for the teller. Logging and outdoors stories find full earthy expression here, as do the Algonkian legends of the manitou in the various forms recalled by Potawatomi, Chippewa, and Menominee. One wizened source on a bar stool related an entire geography of spirits of the rapids and falls of the Wolf system.

In this very spot I heard a ghostly epic that spanned the full distance of the St. Lawrence and the Great Lakes, the full annals of French, English, and American history, and the timeless legends of intertribal battles. The tale was a chilling cocktail of an errant Iroquois spirit, a doomsday device, and a parable of illicit moonshine. Potent stuff, with or without the shot and a beer.

▼ ▼ ▼ ▼ ▼ ▼ ▼ ▼ ▼ ▼ ▼ ▼ ▼ ▼ ▼ ▼ ▼ ▼ ▼ ▼

Marinette

Rail House Brewing Company
2029 Old Peshtigo Road
(715) 732-4646

The rail theme here is not the only reason to toot your whistle. The drive to Marinette is rewarded with four solid house brews: Rail House Silver (a light ale), Gold Rush Red (a caramel malt ale), Coal Car Stout, and Pilsner Honey. Rail House kettles are also used to brew a variety of seasonal ales and a homemade root beer.

Then there's the food. Four appetizers, soups, salads, pasta, steaks, chicken, subs, and an extensive pizza selection. Oh, on Friday, the menu switches over to perch, walleye, cod, shrimp, and whitefish. The dessert selection is growing, too. And Rail House delivers the entire menu within the Marinette, Peshtigo, and Menominee (Michigan) area.

The Rail House may not rank with some of the brand-spanking-new palatial brew pubs of Milwaukee and Chicago, but it has come by its reputation honestly in the hardscrabble Northwoods. Some would say it's the only spot for good beer between Eagle River/Minocqua/Boulder Junction and Green Bay. The Rail House pulls in the travelers and serves as a local rallying point for beer fans.

The cultural milieu is pure transition zone. Marinette keeps one eye on the Fox Valley and the other on the Upper Peninsula of Michigan. Same here with the customers. A conversation here can ramble through the details of a shopping trip to Packer City's Port Plaza, the latest release of the regional music comedy group Da Yoopers, and the latest walleye fishing innovations.

The proposition that good locally brewed beer brings out the nostalgia in folks is borne out here. Among the self-defined regulars I found antique-car restorers, historic reenactors, farm equipment collectors, rendezvous participants, and builders of authentic bark canoes.

Many of my sources pointed to the Rail House as the best beer purveyor betwixt Green Bay and Marquette, Michigan. That compliment damns with faint praise. As hockey fans know, the drive from Green Bay to Marquette is a long one, with plenty of bars but few standouts. There are a few worthy rustics on the Michigan stretch of Highway 41. The Wisconsin passage from the mouth of the Fox to the Oconto and Peshtigo precincts has but a few serviceable bars. Rail House has little competition on the west side of the bay, though it would hold its own in the state's more blessed regions.

▼ ▼ ▼ ▼ ▼ ▼ ▼ ▼ ▼ ▼ ▼ ▼ ▼ ▼ ▼ ▼ ▼

Marshfield

Ron's Brick Tap
317 N. Central Avenue
(715) 384-5535

Any tavern that can certify, as Ron's does, that the tap lines are clean deserves an "A" for effort on behalf of quality draft beer. But customer satisfaction is a major priority here. That could be one reason that the place fills up after work and in the evenings.

The other reasons might have something to do with the customer-tailored beers. Why else would it offer specials on Dempsey's Pale Ale half liter, 16-ounce Budweiser specials, and buck-and-a-quarter Rolling Rock? How else would you account for a four-person order of bottled Guinness, Bass, Corona, and Labatt's Blue? What other explanation could be offered for a large assortment of shorties, including nonalcoholic varieties?

Bartenders at Ron's earn their keep at peak times. They need to deftly sling Rumple Minze shots, Leinie's, and cocktails for a mixed golf, NASCAR, and beer fan crowd. Eight tap lines include some nationals but reserve space for requests, test runs, and flavors of the month. They educate beer palates by introducing folks to the Central Waters brews.

Strangers are not left out at Ron's. The regulars won't let you remain nameless for long. Expect inquiries about your business, politics, and ancestry. If the usual crowd is in fine form, expect some strong opinions about government boondoggles and intrusive regulations.

You might guess that such a place would be ripe with good-natured hyperbole and leg pulling. You would be guessing right. Regulars often play a game of "gotcha" with new faces. In this variation of the game, newcomers are lured into conversation about their interests and accomplishments only to find a rejoinder from the bar from somone who's done it better or faster or knows more about it. This is a funny exercise if done without malice. It's insufferable if the know-it-alls believe they really do know it all.

During my visits the talk tended toward racing and golf. Both crowds are down-to-earth, with no pretense of pro status. Come October, they like a scary story or two. See if you can get someone started on the Upham Mansion tale.

▼ ▼ ▼ ▼ ▼ ▼ ▼ ▼ ▼ ▼ ▼ ▼ ▼ ▼ ▼ ▼ ▼ ▼

Mosinee

Virgie Hunter's Bar
2097 South Road (off Highway X)
(715) 693-3532

Bottles of Point beer for $1. Just about everybody drinks it. Requests for other beers might bring strange looks from the regulars. Enough said.

Those unfamiliar with the area might be fooled by the address. This is as rural a tavern as you will find this side of Wyoming. It's in a belt of rural taverns that starts where Stevens Point's 2nd Street turns into Highway X and runs north toward Schofield. *Be warned: This is a hard place to find unless you pick up the sign on Highway X.*

Alternately known as Virgie's, Hunter's, South Road Tavern, and Virgie Hunter's Bar, the Depression-era building has undergone few changes in 60 years and four different owners. It's still a DNR registration station that ear tags 1,200 deer a year, it still sells hunting licenses. The same Racine, Kenosha, and Milwaukee hunting families visit Grandpop's old spot and sometimes sleep in their trucks in the parking lot.

Fresh produce is available from a large on-site garden. A more or less continuous garage sale is going on out the side door (unless the garage is needed for Packer tailgate parties or Tupperware bingo). Hearty chicken soup and chili are available in the cooler months. The big annual event is a wild turkey and pheasant feed around Labor Day.

Maybe what impressed me the most during my visits was the complete lack of whining that is so common in rural taverns. No conspiracy theories about the DNR or the federal government. No trumped-up complaints about Indians, casinos, and spearfishing. The proprietors are busy having a good time running a bar. Even their terrier happily prances behind the bar in Virgie's.

This spot is a storyteller's delight. I have personally heard more ghost stories, pioneer legends, and contemporary tall tales here than in any other tavern in the state. This is the place where I picked up the leads to such stories as "Polonia's Polutnitsha," "Walter the Warden," and "Deer Camp Dick". The place may seem parochial but usually includes people who have hunted and fished the northern half of Wisconsin and know its back roads well.

One patron told me that an elderly man would appear in the parking lot years ago and sing in Polish to his wife inside. It was a song begging her to come home. The couple are long dead, but the twinkly eyed carrier of the tale said that some nights one can still hear that Polish song.

Oh, by the way, if you happen by at 8 or 9 A.M. on an autumn day you just might find the place packed.

▼ ▼ ▼ ▼ ▼ ▼ ▼ ▼ ▼ ▼ ▼ ▼ ▼ ▼ ▼ ▼ ▼

Peshtigo

The River Pub

French and Front Streets (Highway 41)
(715) 582-2900

The River Pub (known as La Valley's until recently) is an honest-to-goodness after-work bar for locals in an area brimming with hunting and fishing taverns. It also has the best intergenerational mix in this corner of the state. But if you want to hear old-timers spin yarns about the Peshtigo fire, you'd best stop by midafternoon.

The choices here are simple: ice-cold Miller or ice-cold Bud. Well, if you press the point, they might go to a back cooler and drag out an ancient can of Old Style. Despite that, it's still one of the better taverns on the Green Bay–Marinette run. Establishment sensibilities are telegraphed by the house specialty: ice-cold shots of schnapps.

The River Pub has a bit of the feel of a border state bar: slightly hard-edged but definitely not hard-ass, and pleasantly rowdy when in peak form. An earthy utterance or two should not surprise the visitor. Just plug the jukebox and bring up a mix of country, heavy metal, golden oldies, and adult contemporary tunes.

The oval bar is one of the biggest encountered outside of metropolitan areas. It's vintage Formica but remarkably unscathed by cigarette burns. Speaking of cigarettes, the River Pub is definitely a smoker's bar, but with sufficient ventilation to go easy on the noncombustible among us.

My friends swear by the fishing advice they pick up in these friendly confines. According to them, they have run into deepwater devotees, fly-fishers, smelters, river run fanatics, and those who ply the interior muskie lakes. Not to worry, they allow us lowly worm and bluegill types into their exalted space. On my autumn visits the place is more of a hunters' bar, with the blaze orange three deep at the bar. The regulars moan that they are displaced by the downstate crowd. One Fond du Lac wag proudly proclaimed that enough of his work buddies were in the joint to have a quorum for his union local.

▼ ▼ ▼ ▼ ▼ ▼ ▼ ▼ ▼ ▼ ▼ ▼ ▼ ▼ ▼ ▼ ▼ ▼ ▼

Rhinelander

Bugsy's Brown Street Pub and Sports Bar

16 N. Brown Street
(715) 369-2100

Wisconsin "sports bars" seem to encompass everything from the mom-and-pop ten-stool joint with 21-inch TV and Packers pennant to corporate-held big-screen multiplexes. Bugsy's does the TV route with eight screens and ups the ante in its huge space. This is a sports bar in which most sports could be played. And they do play indoor basketball and volleyball here.

So now you're thinking this is one of those glorified pool halls inhabited by Coors Light–drinking 20-somethings. Wrong! Bugsy's has a state-of-the-art four-barrel pub-brewing system. So far they've turned out a wheat, a dunkel, an amber, and a stout—with more on the way. Four additional taps are devoted to micros from around the region. And I suppose the bartenders might be able to rustle up some nationally known facsimile beer for the beer ambivalent.

Open only since July 1998, Bugsy's is well on its way to becoming a regional kind of "House on the Rock" of Northwoods bars that has to be seen to be believed. Local beer fanciers predict a bright future if Wisconsin gets a couple of snowy winters in a row to bring the snowmobilers and cross-country skiers back to the northeast.

The regulars include many recreation-savvy natives. A fishing guide kept my interest for a good hour, even though his story strayed over Hayward way to the famed guide Louis Number One and famed client Ted Williams. While I was thus engaged, my pals got the lowdown on the best housekeeping cottages and boat rentals.

While I mourn the loss of many of the venerable Northwoods taverns, with their yellowed linoleum and their desiccated and dust-fuzzy beef jerky, Bugsy's may represent a new trend that could get younger families back in the taverns. Just like back in those Eisenhower "happy days," only in the twenty-first century.

▼ ▼ ▼ ▼ ▼ ▼ ▼ ▼ ▼ ▼ ▼ ▼ ▼ ▼ ▼ ▼ ▼ ▼

Rhinelander
Labor Temple Bar
2 E. Anderson Street
(715) 362-6750

Here's a feisty little bar that opens at 7 A.M. and closes when there are no thirsty customers left. From the moment I went to work on this guidebook, it was my intent to include a union hall bar. Conventional wisdom would have pointed toward selection of the bigger spots in Racine, Madison, Neenah-Menasha, and Eau Claire. But time and time again my friends in organized labor pointed me toward this Northwoods outpost.

The union hall bar was once a standard part of every mill and factory town. Deindustrialization of many urban cores and flight of many workers to the suburbs left the labor halls as spots used for periodic meetings, not seven-day-a-week community centers. But not so in Rhinelander.

The Rhinelander Labor Temple Bar does a steady business as a tavern while serving that community function. Meetings adjourn to, and informally continue in, the bar.

It's the type of place where candidates for public office have to stop and show a steady gaze and a firm handshake. It's the type of place where traveling union officials must show their mettle by keeping up, beer for beer, with their members and run a tab in lieu of a dues rebate. A segment of Wisconsin's labor movement is in the capable hands of a number of working-class stalwarts, big guys with evidence of their time at the bar hanging unabashedly over their belts. They've seen all the union hall bars from Kenosha to Superior. They say this is the best. You don't want to argue with them.

Conversation is lively and of a populist political bent. If you're hungry, there's pizza. If you're thirsty, there's cold beer (nothing fancy). For itchy feet, there's a band every Saturday night. And if you have high-level recreation needs, there's an indoor golf machine.

Jimmy Hoffa wouldn't drink here, but John L. Lewis would.

▼ ▼ ▼ ▼ ▼ ▼ ▼ ▼ ▼ ▼ ▼ ▼ ▼ ▼ ▼ ▼ ▼ ▼ ▼

ANOTHER ROUND
Wisconsin Breweries

Call for tour and special event information.

Capital Brewery (Garten Brau)
7734 Terrace Avenue
Middleton
(608) 836-7100
www.capital-brewery.com

Cherryland Brewing Company
41 W. Maple Street
Sturgeon Bay
(920) 743-1945

Esser's Cross Plains Brewery
2109 Hickory Street
Cross Plains
(608) 798-3911

G. Heileman Brewing (Old Style/Special Export)
1111 S. Third Street
La Crosse
(608) 782-2337

Gray's Brewing Company
2424 West Court
Janesville
(608) 752-3552
www.graybrewing.com

Harbor City Brewing Company
535 W. Grand Avenue
Port Washington
(262) 284-3118

Hinterland Brewing Company
313 Dousman Street
Green Bay
(920) 438-8050

▼ ▼ ▼ ▼ ▼ ▼ ▼ ▼ ▼ ▼ ▼ ▼ ▼ ▼ ▼ ▼ ▼ ▼

Jacob Leinenkugel Brewing Company
1 Jefferson Street
Chippewa Falls
(715) 723-5558

Jacob Leinenkugel Brewing Company
1515 N. Tenth Street
Milwaukee
(414) 931-3900

Joseph Huber Brewing Company (Berghoff)
1208 Fourteenth Avenue
Monroe
(608) 325-3191

Lakefront Brewery
1872 N. Commerce Street
Milwaukee
(414) 372-8800
www.lakefront-brewery.com

B. T. McClintic Beer Company
136 W. Grand Avenue
Beloit
(608) 365-5596

Miller Brewing Company
3939 W. Highland Boulevard
Milwaukee
(414) 931-2000

New Glarus Brewing Company
Highways W and 69
New Glarus
(608) 527-5850

Nicolet Brewing Company
2299 Brewery Land
Florence
(715) 528-5244

Oconomowoc Brewing Company
750 E. Wisconsin Avenue
Oconomowoc
(262) 560-0388

Pabst Brewing Company
622 E. Vienna Street
Milwaukee
(414) 962-2419

▼ ▼ ▼ ▼ ▼ ▼ ▼ ▼ ▼ ▼ ▼ ▼ ▼ ▼ ▼ ▼ ▼ ▼ ▼

Pioneer Brewing Company
320 S. Pierce Street
Black River Falls
(715) 284-7553

Slab City Brewing Company
W3590 Pit Lane
Bonduel
(715) 758-2337

Sprecher Brewing Company
701 W. Glendale Street
Glendale
(414) 964-2739
www.sprecherbrewery.com

Stevens Point Brewing Company
2617 Water Street
Stevens Point
(715) 344-9310

Tyranena Brewing Company
1025 Owen Street
P.O. Box 736
Lake Mills
(920) 648-8699

Viking Brewing Company
234 Dallas Street
Dallas
(715) 658-1189
www.vikingbrewing.com

Watson Brewing Company
223 Maple Avenue
Waukesha
(262) 896-7766

▼ ▼ ▼ ▼ ▼ ▼ ▼ ▼ ▼ ▼ ▼ ▼ ▼ ▼ ▼ ▼ ▼ ▼

Isadore Street Brewery
200 Isadore Street
(715) 341-1199

Here's the in-town alternative for those of us who feel too old for the student bars on Stevens Point's "square." Be advised, its location adjacent to the UW–Stevens Point campus will expose you to a few peach-fuzz faces. But hey, they're learning about good beer.

The brews came on line in the second half of 1998. At last count five brews were available: a red ale, a lager, an interesting cranberry ale, a stout, and a smooth honey porter. The brews are already out on the tasting fest circuit.

Isadore Street is a roomy spot by Stevens Point standards: seating for 125 at tables, an upstairs bar, and a downstairs bar. The restaurant side is gaining its own following. Finally, a brew pub with prime rib! Thanks. The fish fry is competitive in a town with some good ones (I'm partial to the American Legion Post). Lo and behold, vegetarian entrées as a concession to the tie-dyed crowd from the College of Natural Resources.

This is a good spot to find out what's going on in and about the Point area. The regulars include many people wired into the local arts scene and also a fair sprinkling of winter sports enthusiasts. On my visits I usually manage to share a few brews with members of Point's hiking corps. Nothing better for this old *volksmarcher* than trail advice and directions with your beer.

It is also the best spot for the over-30 crowd to adjourn after a campus concert. If you check in during the day you'll often be able to get tips on what's going on in the student union. For a town that often has some interesting things worth visiting, Point does little to publicize events. Many of my friends in the area tell me they find more about Point in Wausau's papers than in any local source. Izzy Street should be a good antidote to that information drought if the hooked-in crowd continues to frequent this newer kid on the block.

Stevens Point

Witz End

1274 N. 2nd Drive
(715) 344-9045
www.thewitzend.com

Witz End is the place most often mentioned by savvy beer lovers who travel throughout Wisconsin. Stevens Point's role as a statewide conference center and as the second home of the dispersed alumni of UW–Stevens Point are the two main reasons that this old rocking roadhouse boasts a statewide following of microbrew aficionados. At the end of a workday you can find Polish-American potato farmers sampling a new weiss beer and comparing notes on taste with traveling salespeople, DNR wildlife biologists, and graduate students.

Beer literacy is at a high level at Witz End. You'll sometimes see patrons thumbing through brewing industry magazines. The bar has its own website, and the barside computer allows customers to check out microbrew and home brew websites (and band bookings around the state). The novice need not fear beer snobbery. If there's one thing that the people on both sides of the bar at Witz End love more than debating the qualities of fine beer, it's initiating and educating newcomers. If you expect to get the short course on beer appreciation, plan to visit on a weeknight when there is not a band playing. On most Fridays and Saturdays and some Thursdays, this nightspot turns into one of the most lively clubs in the north country.

The house draft specialties are anchored by the full line from Stevens Point Brewing. You will not find as complete a collection of Wisconsin's microbrews anywhere else north of the Fox Valley. Rare bottled beers from throughout the United States are also offered. Witz End management actively tracks down new beers. They visit the microbrew trade shows and travel to breweries to sample new recipes. The benefits to the customer of the active quest for the perfect beer are obvious each time a Witz End bartender talks a customer into trying an unheard-of microbrew.

At this point a confession is in order. Many of my best referrals on good beers and good places to drink them came right here at the lengthy Witz End bar. No kidding. News of the latest suds from New Glarus was the buzz here long before it made the pages of the brewing trade papers. Some of the beer and bar buffs here sent me to spots around the state that I might not have lucked into on my own.

The location makes this a hidden jewel. Follow 2nd Street in Stevens Point north until you pass over U.S. Highway 51 and enter the woods. The Northwoods bar setting is just beyond the city limits.

▼ ▼ ▼ ▼ ▼ ▼ ▼ ▼ ▼ ▼ ▼ ▼ ▼ ▼ ▼ ▼ ▼

Sturgeon Bay
Inn at Cedar Crossing Pub
3rd Avenue and Louisiana Street
(920) 743-4249

This carefully restored 1884 building came into its current reincarnation in 1986. Along the way it picked up a place on the National Register of Historic Sites and added food and drink to its routine in 1989. The pub side of the business came into its own as it expanded its microbrew offerings and began to offer a lighter pub menu distinct from the dining area (which has its own fine reputation).

The result is a restaurant-based bar that stands on its own. Customers, particularly in the busy Door County high season, do indeed come in just for drink and conversation. Draft offerings during my last visit included Paulaner Hefe-Weizen, Samuel Adams Summer Ale, and Bass Ale, though there is some seasonal variation. At last count, the bottled brews tallied up at 34 types, with good representation of imports and micros. Cedar Crossing Pub also has a following for its summer fruit and spirits drinks, often made with local fruit.

It is hard to find the tavern middle ground in Door County. Many good spots are overcome by the crush of tourists. Development and gentrification are claiming others. The Door County taverns of manure on barn boots, the smell of fish entrails, and boatmen's corncob pipes is disappearing. Many of the new spots, as improved as they are from a beer-drinking (and sanitary) perspective, are devoid of local flavor.

The Cedar Crossing Pub represents one aspect of the middle ground. Its downtown business district location helps it draw both travelers and locals. The talk ranges through local land use controversies, real estate prices, and construction industry woes. It is a conversational mix that is on the increase in Wisconsin, but in Door County it is probably more advanced than elsewhere.

One element of the Cedar Crossing Pub operation really impressed me: a congenial midafternoon crowd that makes for good casual companionship for sports or outdoors talk. Many of the best taverns are faced with the lunch and after-work rushes and deal with a lull in between. Some of the shot-and-a-beer joints have afternoon customers who are simply stretching lunchtime into bartime. What is nice about this spot is that it gets sufficient numbers of laid-back travelers to affirm the unhurried mood that befits Sturgeon Bay.

▼ ▼ ▼ ▼ ▼ ▼ ▼ ▼ ▼ ▼ ▼ ▼ ▼ ▼ ▼ ▼ ▼ ▼ ▼

Tomahawk

Pik's Pub
8 W. Wisconsin St.
(715) 453-8966

Locals swear by this nicely renovated and redecorated mainstay. It's earned the approval that goes with doubling up the tavern business with an informal community center status. The result is a Northwoods tavern look without the grime and odors that afflict many taverns. Standard Northwoods tavern decor is spoofed a bit by some unusual wall hangings and a mounted deer's rear end.

Pik's has grown beyond the limited-selection shot-and-beer place by the addition of nine taps. The focus is still on the big-boy corporate brews, but it's gradually teasing palates with Leinie's and Point. All indications point toward the eventual appearance of micros.

Especially if the music crowd holds up. Pik's serves as a multigenre venue for blues, rock, and country. Monday is the blues jam. Wednesdays and Fridays are the primary band nights. Among the entertainment functions are periodic fund-raising dances to buy musical instruments for local students.

The best compliment I can pay Pik's is that it's geared to its local customer base, not some mythic tourist profile of what flatlanders with bucks would like. That is exactly the reason many travelers will like it; it's natural in its place and not pretending to be something it's not. This is the whole lure of the Northwoods tavern, to not be a stranger when you walk in the very first time and to not be surrounded by painfully obvious tourists. Otherwise, you might as well hang out at bars in the Dells and pretend you're in the Boundary Waters.

Tomahawk itself is a fair to middling community for a Northwoods pub crawl, both in the city and in its environs. Some of my hardier associates include it on a tour that takes in Merrill and Marathon City to the south. If you do make that loop, be sure to hit the spots on Highway 107 on the west side of Merrill and the little bunker of a tavern at the junction of Lincoln County highways E and M. Let me know what you find, I've been meaning to stop for years.

▼ ▼ ▼ ▼ ▼ ▼ ▼ ▼ ▼ ▼ ▼ ▼ ▼ ▼ ▼ ▼ ▼ ▼ ▼

ANOTHER ROUND

Beer and Bar Reading

Breweries of Wisconsin, Jerry Apps, University of Wisconsin Press, Madison, 1992.

Cream City Suds, PO Box 1251, Milwaukee, WI 53201, (414) 645-1580 (bimonthly)

Great Lakes Brewing News, 214 Muegel Road, East Amherst, NY 14051, (716) 689-5841 (bimonthly)

Midwest Beer Notes, PO Box 237, Ridgeland, WI 54763, (715) 837-1120 (bimonthly)

Wausau

Scott Street Steak and Pub

124 Scott Street
(715) 842-2424

The conversion from downtown beer and sandwich joint to regional blues and brews spot was done the old-fashioned way: they earned it. Still, the midday traffic has its share of business lunches, and 5 o'clock brings an after-work crowd. The Saturday afternoon crowd, on the other hand, includes many travelers. The regulars include quite a few downtown office workers and government employees. The evenings bring a mix of brew fans, sports enthusiasts, and music lovers. More on the music in a bit.

What brings in the traffic off Highway 51? For starters, eight tap heads with variable offerings of solid Wisconsin microbrews such as Gray's and Sprecher. Summit and Leinie's seasonals often round out the draft selection, along with the locally popular Foster's. The bottled selection usually tallies about two dozen micros and imports, with Gray's having a distinct following among repeat visitors headed toward lakeshore cottages.

Friday and Saturday nights bring out friendly crowds for music. Bookings run toward the blues, with forays into roots rock and fusion. Tony Brown and the Landing Crew make this their northern outpost, as do Otis and the Alligators and Reverend Raven and the Chain Smoking Altar Boys. This is a great tandem visit with Witz End in Stevens Point (and what the heck, with Holly Rocks in Wisconsin Rapids). For good times, these northcentral nightspots hold their own with Madison and Milwaukee.

The regulars include a number of trusty tavern scouts. This is one of the few spots where reliable sources can give you the overview on Wausau's neighborhood taverns. Their field intelligence extends out to nearby Rothschild, Schofield, and Wausau Junction. Rumor has it that they also have the lowdown on hotspots for cribbage and sheepshead.

Scott Street Pub has a comfortable saloon feel with its no-frills interior, bison head over the bar, and old-time pinball machine. Its extensive sandwiches and appetizer menu merits sampling. Don't miss the onion rings.

▼ ▼ ▼ ▼ ▼ ▼ ▼ ▼ ▼ ▼ ▼ ▼ ▼ ▼ ▼ ▼ ▼

Wisconsin Rapids
Holly Rocks
114 Second Street North
(715) 423-1800

A favorite stop for music fans in central Wisconsin, Holly Rocks is also a beer-drinking haven. The seven taps seem like a modest number until you see the handles marked for DAB, Double Diamond Burton Ale, and the Central Waters brews. The bottled selection is impressive, with most regionals and the rarely seen Tennents from Scotland.

This bar has a heart that beats to music, be it blues, classic rock, bluegrass, folk rock, or reggae. The decor follows the theme with suspended and wall-hanging guitars, saxophones, trumpets, banjos, and trombones. A nice collection of vintage concert posters and recording artist photos grace the walls, with nostalgia evoked for the Doors, Hendrix, the Who, Elvis, Janis Joplin, and Bob Marley, among others.

Many music clubs are short on conversation, but not Holly Rocks. On non–band nights the place can be as talkative as any neighborhood tavern. Much of the conversation runs to music. Or should I say life and music? One dueling trivia duo treated me to a run-through of music from the 60s and 70s and its relationship to movies, advertising, television, sports, and high school reunions.

Frequent patrons make the case that there is an emerging folklore of music clubs. In their view the sagas of spaced-out roadies, internal band spats, and seduction by song is the stuff of legends. They made convincing arguments with the archetypes of classic myth, the emerging historical sensibilities of rock and roll, the passage of the five decades since rockabilly, and even a ghost story or two.

Friendly crowds and even friendlier bartenders are the norm. They'll cheerfully steer you to other good taverns (see Huey's Pub and Eatery). A big picture window with a view of a little park and the Wisconsin River lets you watch the world go by. Some might argue that Holly Rocks is a nightclub, but its satisfied beer drinkers say otherwise.

Oh, did I mention that this is one of the cleanest and best-maintained bars I've ever seen? Yet it doesn't come off as a prissy place; the earthy crowd and funky CD collection see to that. It's unusual to hear such mixed conversations about microbrews, guitar chords, sound systems, and album critiques. Check out the odd ashtray collection!

▼ ▼ ▼ ▼ ▼ ▼ ▼ ▼ ▼ ▼ ▼ ▼ ▼ ▼ ▼ ▼ ▼ ▼

Wisconsin Rapids

Huey's Pub and Eatery
140 Second Street North
(715) 421-5665

This entry represents a promise happily broken. My initial resolve was to avoid "clustered" entries lest readers think I failed to travel beyond a few blocks in Madison and Milwaukee. The address above reveals that Huey's is only a few doors away from Holly Rocks. My Wisconsin tavern path might not have crossed Huey's door had not the Holly Rocks crowd insisted on it.

So what did I find? Well, first off, a beer-literate bartender who praised Holly Rocks to the upper stratosphere (tavern owners, a lesson in collegiality here?). Second, another seven taps (the magic number in Wisconsin Rapids?), with Central Waters seasonals heading the lineup. Third, a respectable bottled inventory of about 30 brews. Look for current drink specials, too!

The "eatery" portion of the business also delivers on its promise. An extensive menu offers a downtown blue-collar alternative to the nearby upscale Mead Inn at lunch and dinner. The jumbo shrimp special hit the spot with me, and the oysters on the half shell went down amazingly well at a locale so distant from the ocean. Huey's usually offers about 20 appetizers to go with its lunch and dinner specials.

Huey's and Holly Rocks taken together make up one of those delightful pairings that tavern lovers crave: a one-two tandem on the same block (with other bars nearby). The locals offer this scenario: Huey's for food and a beer and then Holly Rocks for a band and a beer. Who would have thunk it, in quiet Wisconsin Rapids? Huey's deals pretty much with a middle-class family clientele but has not a hint of stodginess. It is great to see families who moved to the bigger house on ten acres come back downtown on Friday night.

Index of Places
and Events

Page numbers in boldface indicate the taverns' main listing.

Index of Places and Events

▼ ▼ ▼ ▼ ▼ ▼ ▼ ▼ ▼ ▼ ▼ ▼ ▼ ▼ ▼ ▼ ▼ ▼

▼ ▼ ▼ ▼ ▼ ▼ ▼ ▼ ▼ ▼ ▼ ▼ ▼ ▼ ▼ ▼ ▼ ▼

▼ ▼ ▼ ▼ ▼ ▼ ▼ ▼ ▼ ▼ ▼ ▼ ▼ ▼ ▼

More Great Titles from Trails Books

Great Wisconsin Restaurants
Dennis Getto

Foods That Made Wisconsin Famous
Richard J. Baumann

Great Minnesota Walks: 49 Strolls, Rambles, Hikes, and Treks
Wm. Chad McGrath

Creating a Perennial Garden in the Midwest
Joan Severa

The Spirit of Door County: A Photographic Essay
Darryl R. Beers

Up North Wisconsin: A Region for All Seasons
Sharyn Alden

The W-Files: True Reports of Wisconsin's Unexplained Phenomena
Jay Rath

The M-Files: True Reports of Minnesota's Unexplained Phenomena
Jay Rath

The I-Files: True Reports of Unexplained Phenomena in Illinois
Jay Rath

Great Wisconsin Walks: 45 Strolls, Rambles, Hikes, and Treks
Wm. Chad McGrath

Great Weekend Adventures
the Editors of Wisconsin Trails

Best Canoe Trails of Southern Wisconsin
Michael E. Duncanson

**County Parks of Wisconsin:
600 Parks You Can Visit Featuring 25 Favorites**
Jeannette and Chet Bell

▼ ▼ ▼ ▼ ▼ ▼ ▼ ▼ ▼ ▼ ▼ ▼ ▼ ▼ ▼ ▼ ▼

The Wisconsin Traveler's Companion:
A Guide to Country Sights
Jerry Apps and Julie Sutter-Blair

W Is for Wisconsin
Dori Hillestad Butler and Eileen Dawson

Walking Tours of Wisconsin's Historic Towns
Lucy Rhodes, Elizabeth McBride, and Anita Matcha

Wisconsin: The Story of the Badger State
Norman K. Risjord

Paddling Northern Wisconsin
Mike Svob

Best Wisconsin Bike Trips
Phil Van Valkenberg

Barns of Wisconsin
Jerry Apps

Portrait of the Past:
A Photographic Journey Through Wisconsin 1865-1920
Howard Mead, Jill Dean, and Susan Smith

Trails Books
P.O. Box 5650, Madison, WI 53705
(800) 236-8088
e-mail: info@wistrails.com
www.wistrails.com